The authors and publisher are not engaged in rendering legal, accounting, financial, or other professional services. If legal, accounting, financial advice, or other expert assistance is required; the services of a competent professional should be sought. This publication is intended to provide general, non-specific information. The advice and strategies contained herein may not be suitable for every individual. It does not cover all the issues related to the topic.

The accuracy and completeness of the information provided here and the opinions stated herein are not guaranteed or warranted to produce any particular results. The authors and publisher specifically disclaim any responsibility for any liability, loss or risk, personal or otherwise, which is incurred as a consequence, directly or indirectly, of the use and application of any of the contents of this book.

The authors and publisher have no personal connection or financial interest in any of the companies, services, or persons mentioned.

Although every effort has been made to ensure the accuracy of the contents of this book, errors and omissions can occur and websites, businesses and information can change, o out of business, or go out of date.

No part of this book may be reproduced, stored in a retrieval system, or transmitted in any form, or by any means, graphic, electronic, mechanical, photocopying, recording, taping, or otherwise, without prior written express consent from the publisher. The exception is brief quotations embodied in critical articles or reviews, which give full credit and reference to this book.

Straightline Publishers, its logo (a light bulb in a black box), the Shortest Distance to Your Goal, *TheSmartestWay*, *TheSmartestWay* to Succeed, *TheSmartestWay* to Succeed Series, and Learn to Succeed *TheSmartestWay* are all trademarks of Straightline Publishers, LLC.

PRINTED IN THE UNITED STATES OF AMERICA

Copyright © 2008 Straightline Publishers, LLC
Library of Congress Control Number: 2009905408
ISBN: 978-0-9824746-0-0

TheSmartestWay™
TO
SAVE

TheSmartestWay™ TO SAVE

Why You Can't Hang on to Money and What to Do About It

Samuel K. Freshman & Heidi E. Clingen

TheSmartestWay™ to Save

Why You Can't Hang on to Money
—and What to Do About It

By Samuel K. Freshman and Heidi E. Clingen

FIRST EDITION, Revised
Publisher: Straightline Publishers, LLC
"The Shortest Distance to Your Goal™"
25876 The Old Road, #313
Stevenson Ranch, California, USA 91381
888.524.8833
Visit our website
www.TheSmartestWay.com

To receive your free eTips,
"TheSmartestWay to Succeed™"
sign up at our website or email us at
Tips@TheSmartestWay.com

What others are saying about
TheSmartestWay™ to Save

"...Money is hard to make and easy to spend or even lose...This book is a must-read for all those consumers wanting to improve their lives through easy-to-follow, sound money management principles."

–Robert Castiglione
President and CEO, LEAP Systems, Inc.

"This is a must-read, especially in this economy. This book is the building block for acquiring true wealth."

–Grant Trauth
Authorized Representative, Wealth Financial Group

"This book reminded me of all the things I knew and had forgotten somewhere along this journey. It made me take an inventory of my life. It also helped me understand that it is never too late to start saving, that I can take it one day at a time, and still make a big difference in the long run."

–Rhonda Gorham
Cosmetics Company Director

"Every individual is the architect of his own fortune."
–Appius Claudius

DEDICATION

We dedicate this book to our offspring,
Sam's four daughters and seven grandchildren
and Heidi's two sons.
May they all learn from this book
and lead a new generation of successful savers.

ACKNOWLEDGEMENTS

Book writing takes teamwork. We are grateful for the generous encouragement of our spouses, Sam's wife Ardyth and Heidi's husband Bill. We're glad for the friends and colleagues who reviewed drafts of the manuscript, including Lee Brown, Jan Brzeski, Heidi Nietert, Elena Schumann, Brenda Freshman, Barbara Stearns-Cochran, and our spouses. Sam is always appreciative of his assistant Cindy Anderson.

This book is so fortunate to have the support of our amazing marketing director, Suzanne Stratton, and our talented book designer/technical pro, Sherry Banz. They deserve special thanks for their dedication.

Along the way, we have been inspired by "penny pinchers" and forewarned by "big spenders." We can never forget our parents and mentors who taught us to be thrifty and make the most of what we had, whether we had a lot or not.

We thank you all.

CONTENTS

PART III: YOUR MONEY AND THE WORLD

INTRODUCTION

"If you would be wealthy, think of saving as well as getting."
—Benjamin Franklin

We live in the richest country in the world, but many Americans are just living "month to month." They have trouble paying their rent or mortgage, their car lease payments, and their credit card bills. Other people simply have a nagging feeling that they should be saving more money.

In our crazy, consumer-driven society, why are some people able to hang on to their money and others aren't? This is a question that has perplexed both of us for many years—even though we are as different from one another as any two people can be. We come from a different education level, social status, and religious background. We are different in our gender and our generation. Nevertheless when we sat down to write this book, we found that we were dedicated to a common goal: to help our readers learn to save hundreds of dollars and live well in tough times.

Two different perspectives

With this book, you get two different perspectives.

Sam's financial and business careers include attorney, banker, real estate investor, college professor, and author. Much of his success is due to guidance from his parents, mentors, and teachers. Sam's father, who was always there for his family and his community, taught Sam not to waste money and to search for value. Like his father, Sam has tried to help others help themselves and has mentored and advised others throughout his life.

Heidi also was raised by thrifty parents. She chose a less-lucrative but satisfying career as an editor and writer. She has helped consumers find value through her work in public relations, retail, editing, teaching, and coaching.

Who needs this book?

Americans have been spending more than they earn. Their out-go is greater than their in-come. If they try to solve this problem only by focusing on earning more money—and don't control where they spend it—they will find themselves "running in circles."

Everyone, no matter his or her income, wants to have more money. That's why this book offers something for everyone-- because everyone can learn to save more money.

Saving money is even better than making money—and much easier. That's because you don't have to go out and earn it—you just keep it!

Small savings over time result in big wealth

They say that the quickest way to double your money is to fold it in half and put it back in your pocket. But seriously, saving increases your money!

Slow and steady saving wins the race. The turtle will outrun the rabbit if the turtle perseveres. Small savings over time are more likely to create wealth than taking big risks. Use the magic of compounding interest to help you. If you keep time on your side, you can create substantial wealth.

Here's an example: If you start by saving just 1% of your income and you bring home (net) $2,000 per month, you would have $20 more per month. Doesn't sound like a lot, right? Here's the good news: If you saved $20 per month for 20 years at an annual rate of 10%, you will have saved about $14,000. At the end of 40 years, you would have saved about $112,000!

Many people don't think about it when they buy something small but overpriced, like a $5 cappuccino. Take a close look at the small treats you buy for yourself. If you gave up just one $5 treat each week, you would have your $20 per month to invest.

It's never too late to start

Small amounts grow to large ones over time, if properly invested. Sam recently gave a donation of bank stock to Stanford University Law School. At the time of the donation it had a market valuation of $100,000. He had owned the stock for a number of years and originally bought it for only $100.

It's not too late to start saving. This book is as important for those who are starting out toward financial independence as those who are way down the path. Of course, the earlier you start the better, as it is much easier to save when you are young and don't have as many commitments and obligations.

No matter where you are in life, you can start now to save and reach your savings goals.

Never stop learning

Heidi's grandmother once told her something that seemed puzzling at the time. She said, "The more I know, the more I know I don't know." When Heidi grew up, she realized that every day she can learn something new. Even the wisest person on the planet can always learn more.

Sam never quits learning. For example, he continues to add items to his list of Principles of Financial Independence, found at the back of this book. He has shared this list with hundreds of people, and it has helped many of them achieve financial security. We suggest that you cut out the list and put it in your wallet or tape it to your mirror. It is kind of a "cheat sheet" map to financial independence.

Practice makes perfect

Now that you have purchased this book, you are entitled to a free subscription to our eTips, "*TheSmartestWay* to

Succeed™." This email blog will encourage you to reach your goals. There are three ways you can get your free subscription: Fax us the form at the back of this book, email us at **Tips@ TheSmartestWay.com**, or subscribe online at our website **www.TheSmartestWay.com**.

Our goal for you

If you are reading this book, you are determined to change the course of your future. We wrote this book so you can learn to enjoy saving money. Instead of gaining pleasure from spending money, you can learn to get pleasure from saving it. By being thrifty, you can save enough money to invest wisely and become financially independent.

We will be writing a book dedicated to investing, as well as other books on how to save and live well.

More inflow than outflow equals happiness

We want you to be happier. If your income is $1,000 a month and you need only $900 per month, you will be happy that you have $100 left over to invest or spend as you wish. You will have avoided debt and managed your income responsibly. On the other hand, if your income is $1,000 and you need $1,100 per month, you will be unhappy and continue to fall behind.

As Charles Dickens wrote in *David Copperfield* more than one hundred-fifty years ago, "Annual income twenty pounds, annual expenditure nineteen six, result happiness. Annual income twenty pounds, annual expenditure twenty pounds and six, result misery."

In other words, if you spend less than you earn, you are more likely to be happy. But if you spend more than you earn, you will be unhappy, because overspending puts you into debt.

As someone once said, "If your outgo exceeds your income, then your upkeep will be your downfall."

Instead, you need to learn to be thrifty.

What it means to be "thrifty"

Perhaps your parents or teachers told you to "save for a rainy day" and "pinch your pennies." That's being thrifty! To be thrifty is to be economical, frugal, spend wisely, and save your money.

Thriftiness isn't just for average people. Some billionaires are thrifty. For example, Jim Walton, son of Sam Walton of Wal-Mart, is worth $18 billion. Nevertheless, he drives a 1999 Chevy pickup. Warren Buffett, worth $57 billion, lives in the same house he bought for $31,500 almost fifty years ago.

You can enjoy life and save at the same time

We all know how to shop and be avid consumers. Unfortunately, many people don't know how to save, invest, and build financial security.

This book will show you techniques to live life fully and cut back on spending at the same time. You will have money left over and live a better life.

Some people spend most of their free time thinking about shopping and how to spend money. Sometimes they think they are "saving" when they shop. Unfortunately, most of the time they are just spending!

Other people devote their spare time to improving their lives, instead of spending money. They visualize how good their life will be when they are finally financially independent. They have learned how to play the game of not spending money—and win. You can, too!

It's not how much you make;
it's how much you keep.

PART I

YOUR MONEY AND YOU

Chapter I

SOME QUESTIONS TO ASK YOURSELF

"Any fool can waste, any fool can muddle,
but it takes something of a man to save,
and the more he saves, the more of a man does it make of him."
—Rudyard Kipling

You become a better man or woman when you handle your money well. To help you do that, throughout this book we will show you how to use *TheSmartestWay*™ questions to help you make the best decisions.

Why are some people rich, but still broke?

You may know someone who makes you wonder, "He makes so much money! Why does he always seem broke?" Believe it or not, it's not difficult to spend beyond your income, even if it's a large income. Why? It's just a matter of more zeros at the end of the balance sheet!

On the other hand, some people with modest incomes have built great wealth. How did they do it? They knew the secret: It's not your salary that makes you rich—it's your saving habits.

It doesn't matter how much you make—or don't make. As we will continue to say throughout this book, "It's not how much you make—IT'S HOW MUCH YOU KEEP."

How do you manage your money?

Saving money is a day-to-day process. Small, daily decisions add up to huge, long-term results. What is your savings goal? Do you have a savings account that would provide for your needs for three to six months? Do you have enough for a down payment on a house? Could you manage your money better?

Here's a little quiz to find out how you're doing. Take a few minutes to answer these questions:

1. Do you take advantage of tax benefits, such as IRAs, 401(k)s, etc.?
2. Do you avoid using check cashing machines or ATM machines?
3. Do you usually pay off your credit cards each month?
4. Do you save at least 10% of your gross income in an emergency fund?
5. Do you avoid late fees and overdraft charges?
6. Do you usually pay with cash instead of credit cards?
7. Do you feel secure about your finances?
8. Are you a comparison shopper who shops with a list?
9. Are other aspects of your life more important to you than shopping?
10. Do you balance your checkbook?
11. Do you buy gifts in an appropriate and cost-effective way? Do you have a plan for supporting yourself with your investments?
12. Do you have control over your budget?
13. Do you make more than you spend?
14. Do you know your total debt? Is it a small amount?
15. Do you resist the temptation to use a debit card?
16. Do you handle your own finances?

17. Do you agree with your children and spouse/significant other on how to handle money?

18. Do you know how you are going to afford retirement?

19. Do you have enough insurance to protect your health, your possessions and your loved ones?

What do your answers mean?

If you answered "no" to two or more of these questions, you need this book!

You need this book to help you think about how you spend your money and to give you techniques to help you make your money work for you. You are reading this book to learn to save and accumulate the money you need to invest and live well. You are reading this book because you believe that there is a way to achieve the financial independence that you have always wanted and that you know you deserve.

What is financial independence?

You are financially independent when you have enough income from your investments to live the lifestyle you want without working another day in your life. This amount of that income depends on you, where you live, and your lifestyle.

For example, if you live in Manhattan, you'll spend more on your life style than you would if you live in a rural area of Montana. If your lifestyle requires a penthouse, you'll spend more than you would if you live in a more modest home. Other factors to consider are your age, your health, and how long you expect to live. Calculate your location, lifestyle, and lifespan and add in variable factors, such as inflation.

Fortunately, financial independence can be created with a relatively small income. You simply need your monthly income to exceed your monthly outgo—for the rest of your life. Financial independence isn't simply a matter of saving and being disciplined. It's also a matter of investing well, a topic we'll explore in a future book. Financial independence is the scenario in which your income from investments supports your lifestyle.

Before you learn to invest, you have to learn to save. Some people get confused about this. You can't invest unless you get out of debt, stay out of debt, and save enough extra funds to invest. This is the path to financial independence.

Who is the servant and who is the master?

As Francis Bacon said, "If money be not thy servant, it will be thy master." P.T. Barnum added many years later, "Money is in some respects life's fire: it is a very excellent servant, but a terrible master." Which do you want to be, the master of your money or its slave?

You may have "toxic debt." Toxic debt is debt that is used to pay for something that produces no income and meets no real need. It also can be debt that produces income, but the income is less than is required to pay off the debt. Toxic debt will mortgage your future and prevent you from reaching your lifelong dreams, such as home ownership or a secure retirement. Toxic debt creates anxiety, stress, and conflict in your relationships.

When you save enough to get out of debt, you will eliminate the need to rotate credit cards, post-date checks, or write uncovered checks. You won't be asking others to help bail you out. You'll be more honest and earn respect from others. Your broken relationships will start to heal. Instead of worrying about money, you'll be able to give your job and your loved ones the attention they deserve.

When you rid yourself of toxic debt, your mind and body will improve. You'll suffer fewer stress-related illnesses. You'll sleep well. The discipline you exercise in controlling your money will create new "mental muscles" will help you establish a healthier lifestyle, both financially and physically.

To eliminate toxic debt may be difficult. However, you can do it if you use self-control. This little phrase can encourage you: "If you save your money, it will save you."

What are your priorities?

People can be strongly influenced by what they read in magazines and what they see on television. The media can turn people's priorities upside down.

Here are some questions to ask yourself: Do you own your possessions? Or do your possessions own you? Do you fill your life with things that have real value for you and truly enrich your life? Or are your possessions stealing the time, affection, and attention that you should be giving to your loved ones?

Your relationships with your friends and loved ones should be your top priorities. They enrich your life more than all the money in the world ever could. Nevertheless, your money situation affects your relationships. When you work to provide a home, college, and retirement for your loved ones, you are keeping your relationships your top priority.

To be truly successful, get your priorities, your relationships, *and* your money in alignment.

What is the meaning of success?

Your definition of success is personal. It's a matter of choices. We live in a great country. Here, we all can decide what we want to achieve and make it happen. Freedom is a wonderful thing to have and it's a wonderful thing to give. The more financial resources you have, the more you will be able to share success and freedom with others.

You need to learn to save and spend wisely to be successful in life. If you have money, you'll get where you want to go, faster.

The most popular question

For over thirty years, Sam has lectured at various universities and colleges on Principles of Financial Independence and conducting mentoring programs for master's degree students and professionals. The question people ask Sam most often is, "What is the secret to becoming financially independent?" He reminds them that small sums, saved and invested, become large funds through the miracle of compound interest. His answer always is, "It's not how much you make—IT'S HOW MUCH YOU KEEP.

> *It's not your income that makes you rich;*
> *it's your savings habits.*

Chapter 2

WHY ARE YOU IN DEBT?

*"Money talks
—but all mine ever says is 'good-bye.'"*
—Anonymous

Are you in debt? Does the amount of your debt make you uncomfortable? Have you ever thought about why you are in debt?

We are living in a consumption-drunk society that operates on the mistaken conviction, "I want what I want—so I should have it now!" We are weakened by advertisements that urge us to buy things we don't need. For years, credit and debt have been relatively easy to acquire, so we are accustomed to deep debt. These are some of the destructive influences that have kept our dreams out of reach.

Know how you got into this situation

Examine your thinking to discover the motivation for your spending habits. For example, you may overspend due to feelings of blame, resentment, guilt, and low self-esteem. Consider some of these possibilities that may cause you to be in debt:

- You may be overspending to impress others. You may lack the confidence to say to your family and friends, "I want a new [car, house, widget], but I need to wait until I can afford it."

- You may be purchasing gifts you can't afford in order to buy your spouse/significant other's love or your children's gratitude and forgiveness. You may be substituting gifts for love. Perhaps your parents tried to buy your love when you were young.

- You may feel that since you work hard, you deserve to reward yourself. The media is full of messages encouraging these indulgences.

- You may be feeling lonely or unfulfilled. Face it, it's easier to go out and buy something new rather than to build relationships or reach for your dreams.

- You may be addicted to shopping. Perhaps your constant need to go shopping is a way to distract yourself from doing what you should be doing to improve your life and actually increase your self-esteem.

- You may be worried about the world's problems and determined to just "live for today," no matter what the cost.

- Your family may have taught you to overspend. Childhood programming is difficult to change unless you acknowledge it.

- You may be convinced that debt is inevitable, that you are never going to get ahead anyway, so why try?

- You may still be rebelling against parents who "pinched their pennies." To compensate for a deprived childhood, you may drive yourself to acquire things that you feel you deserve.

Look at this list and think about why you are in debt. If you don't understand it, you can't control it. If you don't deal with your deeper motivations, it wouldn't matter how much money you had; you would still overspend. You need to get your thinking right before you can get your finances right.

Understand the mechanics of money

To be truly successful financially, you need to save, spend wisely, and understand the mechanics of money. You need to know where it all goes--whether it's disappearing through inflation, taxes, or your weakness for the influence of corporate advertising.

If you can anticipate the factors that take away your money, you can outsmart these situations by planning ahead. Then you can save enough to invest successfully and reach financial independence.

Plan for the speed bumps on the road of life

The best policy is to expect the best, but plan for the worst.

Life can come at you fast sometimes. Murphy's Law says, "Anything that can possibly go wrong—will!" Sam adds, "Murphy was an optimist!"

Job loss, divorce, illness, disability, and accidents create financial emergencies when you don't have enough funds set aside. What you need is a funding buffer, a savings account that protects you like the bumper on your car.

Don't make assumptions

Some of you have wealthy parents or family members. You may expect to receive an inheritance someday. Consider the possibility that "your" money might not eventually reach you. It could be eroded by unexpected long-term medical care needs, estate taxes, or financial or economic downturns.

Perhaps your inheritance is only hinted at, implied, or assumed. Perhaps you might have a "falling out" with a family member. Perhaps your relatives might remarry and/or live much longer than expected.

Do you know specifically when the inheritance will arrive? Do you know exactly how much it will be? In any case, don't spend it before you get it. "Don't count your chickens before they're hatched" is a phrase Heidi heard from her mother many times. This is a good motto for all of life's expectations.

Later we will show you that a windfall such as an inheritance is not for spending; it is creative capital to invest. Windfalls are an extra boost toward reaching financial independence.

"Put your own oxygen mask on first"

We all want to help those who are near and dear to us. Nevertheless, we must take care of ourselves first, before we can help others.

You can't help others if you are in trouble yourself. Airplane flight attendants remind us, "Put your own oxygen mask on first." This well-known phrase is a good way to remember this principle.

Help yourself first and keep your own money safe. You can help others later, after you have reached your own financial goals.

Reduce money stress

You may be stressed out about your money. Ask yourself if you are doing the following:

- Listening to media hype and deceptive advertising
- Signing up for too many credit cards, debit cards, and lines of credit
- Running up the balances on your credit cards
- Consolidating your debt with a disreputable credit counselor
- Buying a more expensive car, wardrobe, or home than you can afford

Money stress can cause you to make choices that you may regret later. Usually, decisions made under stress are not good decisions.

Be happy with fewer things

When you see something you would like to have, ask yourself, "Do I really need to own it--just because I like it?" If you don't need it, don't buy it.

A life of simplicity and freedom from endless material wants can be liberating. An added bonus is that you will simplify your finances and have more money to invest in things of lasting value.

Develop the habit of saving

Your savings can start small, but the rewards of saving are infinite. Find the inner motivation, the genuine desire to change your life for the better. Energize your commitment to change by visualizing the improved life you will enjoy.

Einstein defined insanity as "doing the same thing over and over again and expecting different results." So do something different—start saving!

It's not what your money makes of you;
it's what you make of your money.

Chapter 3

GET FREE FROM DEBT

*"If we command our wealth, we shall be rich and free.
If our wealth commands us, we are poor indeed."*
—Edmund Burke

If you command your wealth, you command your life. Here are some ideas to help you become debt free so you can start to preserve your wealth and get your life back.

Cleanse yourself of toxic debt

Toxic debt is poison. It constricts your financial wellbeing by burdening you with interest payments, fees, and dependence on further debt. Toxic debt also prevents you from investing and achieving financial independence.

For many people, their debt is working against them. They may not know it, but they are swimming against a rip tide of toxic debt that is pulling them down. It's difficult to keep from sinking lower, a little more each day. Too often, it's just easier to say, "I'll just put this on my credit card."

You need to cleanse your life of this debt.

This is simple, but not easy. You may be enmeshed in your lifestyle of "living large" while racking up debt. You somehow may be keeping up with your friends, family, and neighbors.

Realize, however, that they may be spending beyond their means just like you. You could all be silently sliding down the road to ruin together.

In any case, if you keep up your current level of debt, you will not have enough money left over to invest in your future and create financial independence for yourself. That's why we will show you how to control your debt in Chapter 9.

Protect your credit rating

You may be handling those "easy, low, minimum payments" every month. But what if something happened that made it difficult to make those payments? What if you lost your job or lost your roommate? What if you became injured, sick, or divorced? What if the interest rate on your credit was increased?

If you are late on your payment, the credit card company has the right to "dial down" your credit rating. This is very serious. A low credit rating, also known as your credit score, could prevent you from getting a loan or buying a home in the future.

Find a role model

Is there someone you know who handles their money well, who has money left over at the end of the month? Maybe it's a friend, relative, co-worker, church member, or club member. Tell them that they have been an inspiration to you. Find out if they will give you some advice or mentor you and support your efforts to do better with your money.

Ask someone to hold you accountable

There is nothing like accountability to help eliminate bad habits. Find a mentor, someone you trust to hold you accountable. Tell that person your savings goal. It could be, "I'm going to buy only one latte per week this month," or "I'm going to put $100 in my savings account at the end of each month," or "I'm going to pay off all my credit cards by the end of the year."

Give that person permission to ask you periodically if you achieved your goal. Write the goal down on a piece of paper, tape it to your bathroom mirror, and look at it when you brush your teeth twice a day. This helps you set the goal in your mind as a top priority.

Play the Game of Not Spending Money

Make not spending money into a game. You need to win the game of Not Spending Money and outsmart your compulsion to spend.

Like any game, when you earn points, you feel a thrill of satisfaction. This game should be no different. Therefore, we suggest that when you reach each goal, give yourself an appropriate reward, based on how hard the goal was to achieve. To get motivated, think of some rewards you could give yourself that would be fun or feel good—but would not cost money. Some examples of no-cost rewards are a hike in the woods, a soak in the bathtub, or a picnic under the stars.

Share your goals and your planned rewards with your loved ones and your mentor. They will encourage you while you strive to reach your goals and celebrate with you when you reach them. But be careful--don't spend yourself back into debt when you celebrate!

Dream of the day when you will be able to pass on the help your mentor gave to you, when you can help someone else who has become ensnared in debt but wants to break free.

Become more introspective

Don't let your financial situation make you crazy with anxiety. Instead, sit down in a quiet place and fearlessly and honestly confront yourself about how you handle your money. Admit your weaknesses, bad habits, and temptations.

Realize that you are not able to outspend your friends, family, and neighbors. Face your fears of being rejected by others if they were to find out about your true financial situation. Ask yourself *TheSmartestWay*™ question: "Why do I care so much about what other people think of me?" Actually, you may be thinking more about them than they are thinking about you!

Now, ask yourself, "How can I use my money to help myself and my loved ones in a way in which I can be proud?" By handling your money the right way, you will set a positive example of financial responsibility for others. You may even earn their respect. As an added bonus, you will have much less anxiety.

Make your financial life more manageable

Money has become so very complicated. Make it simple again. Here are some suggestions: decide who—you or your spouse/significant other—should handle the household finances. Agree that they will be the money gatekeeper.

You could also consider hiring a bookkeeper for a modest fee if neither of you is good at balancing your checkbooks. The bookkeeper's fee could be less than the overdraft fees and late charges you cause yourself.

Understand the Money Machine

The Money Machine is Heidi's name for "big money." Massive financial institutions, powerful financiers, and global political structures control how much of the world's money operates. The Money Machine is the mover and shaker of global finance. It has functioned rather freely because, until recently, the public has been generally unaware how it works.

On a consumer level, the Money Machine offers a number of services to help customers handle their finances. Here's an example: Banks and credit unions design their savings and investment services such as ATMS and products, such as debit cards, to offer convenience to the customer. Have you ever noticed how there is always some kind of cost for convenience? One of the costs of ATMS and debit cards is overdraft fees.

These fees are automatically deducted from your account if you overspend. Unfortunately for customers, these fees add up to tens of billions of dollars of profits for financial institutions every year.

Try to be conscious of how the Money Machine affects your life. Be vigilant. Don't relinquish control of your money freely. Otherwise, if you're not careful, your money will sprout wings and fly away, only to be sucked back into the vast void of the Money Machine.

Avoid debit cards

Debit cards can encourage loss of control of your funds. If you and your spouse/significant other withdraw from the same bank account on the same day, you easily could become overdrawn and bounce checks all over town. It may be better to have separate accounts or mutually agree before each purchase. A cash-and-carry system helps this problem, too.

Learn about "positive debt"

Debt can either work for you or against you. Some kinds of debt can work for you. If a debt is increasing your cash flow, it is called "positive" debt.

For example, you could use a low-interest rate loan to pay off high-interest debt. Say you have a large debt on a credit card that charges you 18% interest. If you could get a loan from the bank or credit union at 8% interest and pay the credit card off, you would have automatically saved yourself 10% in interest payments. This could be a significant savings.

Here's another example: Say you have $10,000 in the bank or credit union earning 3% interest. You also have a loan for a car on which you are paying 6% interest. It makes sense to take money that is giving you 3% and use it to pay off a loan that is costing you 6%.

In other words, if you have debt or a loan at a higher interest rate and you can get another loan at a lower interest rate, you can pay off the higher rate loan with the lower rate loan. Or you can use a loan at a lower interest rate to buy something that earns you a higher interest rate. Either way, you can save large amounts of money in interest payments that you didn't have to pay.

Control your money consumption

Some people go over their budgets very carefully each month—others just go over them! It's easy to spend more than you have. The question is how do you get your budget under control?

One technique is to think of spending money like eating food. Steal a tip from people who lose weight. Dieters are advised to keep a "daily food diary" to monitor what they eat. Do the same thing with your money consumption. Keep a daily money diary. This will show you how much money you are spending each day, when, and where.

To keep your record, you can put a small piece of paper in your wallet or carry a notepad in your purse. Every time you buy something, jot down the details of the purchase. You could also enter it in your PDA. Yes, it's inconvenient to make a note of every purchase. But that's part of why this technique works. It makes you stop and think each time you buy something. You may even be less eager to make purchases because you know that you will have to log the purchase into your daily money diary.

To break a habit, such as the habit of spending unconsciously, you have to first notice when you are doing it. A "daily money diary" helps you notice when you are spending so you can learn to control your behavior.

The daily money diary also helps you see exactly how much you spend on those little "budget-busters" every week. Do this for a month. You'll be surprised to see where your money goes. Then use your daily money diary to help you establish a monthly budget that realistically meets your needs.

Keep a small wallet

Here's another trick related to dieting. You may have noticed that if you have a larger plate, you tend to put more food on it. Also, if you put a large portion on your plate, you tend to eat it all!

The same concept of the size of your dinner plate applies to the size of your wallet. Keep a small wallet. Don't carry more cash with you than you need.

As an experiment, for one week reduce by 20% the amount of cash you usually keep in your wallet. At the end of the week, you will probably have managed just fine. Now you can save that 20% every week. It will start to add up!

Get on a cash-and-carry basis

It's easy to get "hooked" on credit cards. Credit card addiction can sneak up on you. Before you know it, you may start "tossing down your plastic" several times a day. It's not until you get your monthly credit card statement that you finally realize what you are doing to yourself.

Extra credit cards in your wallet can make you feel like you have extra money. Credit is very, very expensive money. Use it only in an emergency. If you can't pay the card off at the end of the month, you can't afford the purchase. Try to remind yourself, "It's not money; it's plastic—and it's toxic debt!"

Here's how to get on a cash-and-carry basis: First, list all the things you can use cash to purchase, such as groceries, haircuts, lunches, gas for your car, clothes, entertainment, etc. Second, put the cash you have allocated for each category for that month in its own labeled envelope.

Third, resolve to quit using debit cards, checks, and credit cards. You and your spouse/significant other must promise each other that you will not use your credit card anymore. The only conditions in which you would use the credit card are (1) if it is a planned purchase that you both agree on together, or (2) if you are 200% committed to paying off the entire balance that month.

Be sure to give yourself a small weekly spending allowance for occasional treats such as beverages and grooming items. But once that weekly allowance is spent, you must wait until the next week to treat yourself.

When you get "unhooked" from credit card addiction and use cash for your purchases, your friends will be curious. They will wonder how can you be so prepared and disciplined to be on a cash-and-carry basis. Simply explain to them that you are living within your budget and they can do it, too.

Control your thinking

Debt is a state of financial insecurity that can make you anxious. Freedom from debt is a state of financial security that makes you feel great!

Your goal of financial freedom will seem impossible until you learn to control your thinking and start believing in yourself and your ability to overcome your circumstances. To survive in today's tumultuous financial environment, you must resolve to thrive, not just survive.

Affirm that you can "beat the system" that has tried to beat you. Systematically pay down your debts, save for investments, and start enjoying more peace of mind and confidence. Adopt the attitude that you can get yourself back on track and win the game of Not Spending Money.

Control your saving

Formulate a realistic plan to save, even if it's just a few dollars a month. Starting out small is okay. The goal is to develop the habit of saving. Gradually increase the amount you save. Most people should be saving at least 10% of each paycheck for an "emergency" fund.

The larger the savings, the larger the results. Strategic, disciplined savings can have enormous, long-term benefits.

Visualize your future

It's liberating to save enough money to be debt free and to invest. It's such a relief to be free from the anxiety and guilt of being in debt. Here's how to visualize yourself taking back control of your life. When you have a few quiet moments, close your eyes and imagine yourself accomplishing the first small, easy steps.

What will it feel like to look at your bank or credit union account balance and see a large amount? What will it feel like to see your billing statement with zero due? What will it feel like to cut that credit card in half? Let yourself feel the pride and relief. Remind yourself often what it will feel like to be debt free.

It's not how much you own;
it's how little you owe.

Chapter 4

"HAVE-TO," "WANT-TO," AND "NEED-TO" MONEY MANAGEMENT DECISIONS

"If your desires be endless,
your cares and fears will be so too."
—Thomas Fuller

Learn to want only what you truly need. Here's how. Every decision can be placed in one of three categories: "have-to" decisions, "want-to" decisions, or "need-to" decisions. First you need to be able to separate a want from a need. Learn to distinguish between something you need in order to survive and something you simply desire.

Understand "have-to" decisions

"Have-to" decisions are decisions about what someone else wants us to do, or which you think you need to do because someone else expects you to do it. Do you worry too much about what other people think about you? You may have told yourself, "I 'have to' buy that new car or house—or I will feel embarrassed!"

Sadly, it's human nature to judge others by their possessions, rather than by their character. You may be judged critically by others. Nevertheless, you alone are responsible for your finances, despite other people's criticisms.

Whenever you hear yourself think, "But I 'have to'!" stop and ask yourself, "Do I really 'have to'? What game am I trying to win--and is the game winnable?"

You may have heard the phrase, "He who dies with the most toys wins." Unfortunately, there is no way to win that game. Why? There will always be someone who has more toys than you. The game that you can win is this one: save, invest, and get rich. Here is the irony: If you're focused on trying to appear wealthy, you're actually ruining your opportunity to become wealthy.

Understand "want-to" decisions

The next level of money motivations is "want-to" decisions. These are decisions we make when we buy things we want. We want these things for our personal pleasure, comfort, temporary satisfaction, or to relieve stress or disappointment. You may have said to yourself, "I knew I couldn't afford it, but I wanted it, so I bought it anyway." Look at "want-to" decisions carefully. They are seldom rational.

To spend on "wants" cripples your savings plan and detours your path to wealth.

Understand "need-to" decisions

The last and most important level of motivation is "need-to" decisions. What is necessary to meet your life goals and care for your loved ones? You need to pay for your basic need of food and shelter (appropriate in relation to your income) and to save for investment, retirement, your children's education, and unexpected emergencies. You probably have life goals that require investment in yourself for future reward.

Everyone has had the unpleasant surprise of major appliances that break down, cars that need repairs, or dental work that just can't wait. A relative may need long-term medical care someday. Medical expenses can crack your own retirement nest egg if your health deteriorates. Health care costs are rising all the time, and people are living longer. Put all these possibilities together and you can see that saving your money wisely is a "need to" decision.

To categorize a purchase as a real "need," you must have a clear understanding of your own definition of "have-to"s, "want-to"s, and "need-to"s. A good test is to ask yourself *TheSmartestWay™* questions: "Is this the best use of my money? Can I live without this? Do I really need this in order to improve my life?"

Keep your real needs uppermost in your mind. This will help you resist the "have-to"s and "want-to"s and help you focus on the "need-to"s.

Don't catch "the wants" virus

Don't have endless wants. Constant longing for something you can't have or shouldn't have can make you miserable. Heidi calls this misery "the wants" virus. You have "the wants" virus when you say too often, "If only I had [fill in the blank]."

Even if you finally get that thing you want, you may find it isn't what you really wanted after all. You've heard the warning, "Be careful what you wish for—you might get it."

Develop "savings muscles"

Everything you do throughout your day is based on inner decisions. To make the best decisions, ask yourself *TheSmartestWay™* questions: "What are my real needs? How should I be meeting them?"

Exert your energy to reach your savings goals and take action that will help you achieve them. Exercise your "savings muscles." Like exercise, the more often and continuously you do something, the easier it becomes and the stronger you become.

Analyze your money messages

Most of us have subconsciously adopted various attitudes about money. These money messages are "truths" we tell ourselves, without carefully analyzing them. Some examples of these money messages are "I don't know how to save because my family never did, or never could," "I'm going to just spend all my money while I can and after I'm gone, everyone else can sort it all out," "I avoid managing my money because it's too boring, too hard, too overwhelming or too confusing," or, "I would rather read the back of a cereal box than my bank statement."

To change the experiences you have with money, you have to change your attitude about money. To take control of your attitude is to take responsibility of your financial life and learn to control your financial destiny.

You may have subconscious prejudices against people who have more money than you have. You may have been taught that "rich people think that they are better than everyone else," "rich people are not to be trusted," or, "rich people are unhappy because money can't buy happiness." The fact is, people with wealth are no worse, or no better, than anyone else.

Analyze your own money messages and see if they might be holding you back on your path to wealth.

Understand your money motivations

How you think about money may depend partly on when you were born. People raised during the Great Depression of the 1930s think differently about money than those raised during the Baby Boomer Generation. The Generation Xers and the Millennial Generation also have their own approach to money.

Regardless of our age or how we were raised, emotions can influence how we use our money. If you're insecure, it's natural to buy things to try to gain acceptance. If you're troubled by a relationship, you may be tempted to try to "buy" love with the "perfect" gift.

If you are proud, you may vow to yourself, "Someday, I'll show them!" If you're vengeful, you may secretly desire to hurt others or shame them with your money.

Examine the emotions behind your money motivations. If you misuse your money, you're only hurting yourself, not others.

Be reasonable about your money decisions

Let's face it. Some money decisions aren't reasonable. A recent study found that many people aren't interested in learning how to save and invest. Why wouldn't people want to learn how to have more money?

One reason might be is that we live in a seductive "buy now, save later" culture. Manufacturers of products spend massive funds on research to help them convince us to buy their products. We are exposed to hundreds of marketing messages every day in magazines and movies, on billboards, television, and the Internet. Advertisements are everywhere, from park benches and shopping carts to the sides of buildings.

Too many people are obsessed with the "art of the sale," the all-consuming hobby of shopping—what they bought, where they bought it, how much they paid for it.

Unfortunately, their money could eventually disappear altogether—and they won't even know where it went—if they continue to focus on spending their money instead of saving it.

Remember Sam says, "It's not how much you make—IT'S HOW MUCH YOU KEEP." Resolve to be free yourself from the pressure of our culture. Learn to resist the "have-to"s and the "want-to"s, and buy only the "need-to"s.

It's not the "have-to"s or "want-to"s;
it's the "need-to"s.

Chapter 5

BE CREATIVE AND SAVE MONEY

"The habit of saving is itself an education;
it fosters every virtue, teaches self-denial,
cultivates the sense of order, trains to forethought,
and so broadens the mind."
—T.T. Munger

I f you want something badly enough, you often can find a way to compromise and get it inexpensively and yet effectively. You can learn to be creative about getting what you want. Here are some examples from Sam and Heidi's lives.

You can have a room with a view

When Sam first started practicing law, his goal was to have an office in Beverly Hills. But he couldn't find "a space for services" arrangement--to exchange his legal time in exchange for office space. (This was how most young lawyers started back then, when they did not have enough money to rent an office.)

He did, however, find a firm that had a large, windowless storeroom. It rented for only $25 a month, compared to the average rate of $100 a month for an office with a window. When he bought his office furniture, he asked the store decorator for advice. The decorator suggested installing drapes across one of the walls to give the impression that a window was behind the drapes. Sam followed this advice and thus created a presentable office within his budget.

From this experience, Sam demonstrated that sometimes you can have what you want (at least almost!) if you are willing to be creative.

You can have a dream

While studying at Stanford University, Sam and his roommate dreamed about a tour of a major motion picture studio. In those days, the only way you could get onto a movie studio lot was if you knew someone who would give you a private tour. Sam's roommate's mother worked for a studio and she tried to get the two boys a tour, but she couldn't.

Still, Sam was determined to figure out how to get a tour. He wrote a letter to the top executives of each of the three major studios in Hollywood. The letter explained that he was writing an article for the Stanford University newspaper about the influence of motion pictures on college students. He asked for an interview with each studio head and a tour of their studio. All three studios sent him back a pair of private studio tour passes. The heads of two of the studios each granted him a personal interview. He sent them copies of the article after it was published and received access to the studios again the next year.

From this experience Sam learned, "If you can dream it, you can do it."

You can strategize and negotiate

Here's something most people don't realize: you can negotiate with your home insurance company. For example, you can often negotiate with the insurer on the relocation reimbursement for living expenses.

Many home owners' insurance policies have a "living expense" benefit. Here's an example of when you might use that benefit: Your home could require repairs that may be paid by your insurance policy. In that event, you may need to move out of your home while the problem is being repaired. If that happens, your insurance policy may cover reimbursement for your living expenses during that time, up to a certain amount.

A friend of Sam's had an 8,000 square foot home in Malibu that was destroyed in a wildfire a few years ago. He wisely had purchased sufficient coverage on the home. The owner was able to prove that the rental fee for a similar home would be $10,000 a month. It was estimated that it would take eighteen months to replace the destroyed home. Thus, the insurance company was obligated to pay $180,000 in reimbursements for living expenses ($10,000 per month for eighteen months).

Many of the man's neighbors had similar losses from the fire. They chose to use their relocation reimbursement for expensive hotel rooms to live in while their homes were being rebuilt. They spent those months living luxuriously, but in the end they had nothing to show for it.

Sam's friend had a better idea. He met with the insurance company and negotiated a settlement of $150,000 in cash for his living expenses. He then bought a trailer for $20,000 and placed it on his lot while the house was being rebuilt.

He put the remaining $130,000 into investments. These investments would produce a $10,000 per year income for him for the rest of his life. As part of his estate, he will pass on the $130,000—which at the time of his death will have grown into about $1,000,000—to his grandchildren.

Sam's friend and his wife had worried that it might be difficult to live in a 800-square-foot trailer for a few months while they waited for their house to be rebuilt. To their surprise, they found the smaller quarters to be rather convenient.

You can have special events on a budget

We believe the special events in your life—whether anniversaries, bar mitzvahs, first communions, baptisms, quinceaneras, or weddings—can be fabulous, without depleting your savings account.

About twenty-five years ago, Heidi and her first husband-to-be decided to get married. They were on college student budgets, but they were determined to create an elegant wedding.

First, Heidi spent $100 on satin, lace, and ribbon for her wedding gown. Her mother-in-law-to-be sewed the gown as her wedding gift. The groom's tux was $50. The best man and the maid of honor agreed to wear their own formal clothes. The invitations and stamps cost $100. The minister's fee was $50. The simple wedding cake cost $50. The case of champagne cost $50.

The day before the wedding, Heidi bought $50 of fresh roses at the discount flower market to use in her bouquet, the boutonnieres, the floral headpiece for her veil, and to adorn the cake. The couple had found the perfect wedding/reception site: a small amphitheater of trellises covered in roses, overlooking the San Francisco Bay, which cost only $50 to rent for the day. The roses were in bloom in June, so there was no need to buy more flowers. The grand total for their entire wedding was only $500. Nevertheless, they received many compliments.

While prices are higher now than they were then, the total cost for a small but elegant wedding could be less than $2,000, depending on your priorities. A lovely gown can be bought or created for less than $500. You could spend another $500 on the bride's accessories or a bridesmaid's dress. With the remaining $1,000, you could spend an average of $100 for the invitations and stamps (print them yourself), $100 for the groom's tuxedo, $100 for the wedding/reception site, $100 for champagne, $100 for the cake, $200 for flowers and bouquets, and $300 for the minister's fee.

Remember, your wedding doesn't "have to" cost a small fortune. If you are choosing between a down-payment on a home and a lavish wedding, choose creative simplicity for your special day. The day will be remembered with pleasure and pride.

It's not what you do;
it's how you do it.

Chapter 6

DEVELOP DISCIPLINE IN YOUR PERSONAL FINANCES

*"A man's treatment of money is the most decisive test
of his character—how he makes it and how he spends it."*
—James Moffatt

As W. Somerset Maugham sadly pointed out, "The unfortunate thing about this world is that the good habits are much easier to give up than the bad ones." Someone else observed, "Bad habits are like a comfortable bed, easy to get into, but hard to get out of."

We all know that it takes discipline to handle money wisely. Nevertheless, if you develop good money habits, your money will be good to you.

Get a good return on your money

Everyone wants to get a good return on their money. How would you like to make 10% to 20% on your money? Here's an easy way: pay off your credit cards! If you don't have to pay your credit card interest rates of 10% to 20%, it's the same thing as saving or earning that money. Don't be one of the vast numbers of credit card holders who are paying interest on their balances.

Verify your expenses

Open up each bill when it arrives and analyze each bank and credit card statement to confirm its accuracy. Put each bill in its own file or envelope.

For your checking account, use check stubs that make a copy of the checks you write. This helps you balance your checkbook because it provides a copy of all the checks you wrote, in case you forget to note it in your records.

Avoid ATMs

Avoid automated teller machines. ATMs are convenient, but convenience costs. If you use an ATM at a bank or credit union branch that isn't your own branch, you may be charged a fee for using that ATM. Many ATM fees are rising; they can add up fast. The cure for ATM dependency is to plan ahead and go to your bank or credit union during bank hours.

Don't hide your spending behind "saving"

When you buy something that is a "want" rather than a "need," it is not a savings, even if you used a coupon or got it on sale. You didn't really "save" money, you spent money. This reminds us of the story of the spouse who proudly returns home from a shopping trip and tells his or her mate how much money all the sales at the store "saved" them. The response from the mate is, "If we saved so much, why do I feel so broke?"

We encourage you to use coupons and shop at sales. Just don't let yourself get carried away by all the spending opportunities.

Earn extra money

To reach your goal of having extra money, you may need to explore beyond your "comfort zone" and look for new ways to make more money.

Weekend or evening jobs can supplement your earnings. You can share your home or apartment with a friend, relative, or tenant and split expenses with them. For extra spending money, you can offer to baby sit, house sit, pet sit, walk dogs, run errands, or provide other occasional services.

Sleep better at night

There is an old saying, "Make good habits and they will make you." The suggestions in this book work. Pretty soon, your new savings habits will become easier and you will start to see how they make good things happen in your life. Plus, the peace of mind you will gain will help you sleep better at night.

It's not your habits that control you;
it's you who controls your habits.

Chapter 7

OUR BEST MONEY ADVICE: END PROCRASTINATION

*"Many people take no care of their money
'til they come nearly to the end of it,
and others do just the same with their time."*
—Goethe

A law of physics states, "A body in motion tends to stay in motion; a body at rest tends to stay at rest." You may feel indecisive, not knowing how to start saving. Your indecision may be paralyzing you. But choosing to do nothing is still a choice with consequences. Procrastination—doing nothing—can hurt you. Procrastination could cause you to lose out on opportunities that could benefit the rest of your life. The following suggestions can help you overcome procrastination in your savings program.

Identify your favorite excuses

We all have our favorite excuses for why we can't or won't do what we know we should do. For example, we all know we should "eat less and exercise more." It's a simple concept. Why is it so easy to find good excuses not to do it? We tell ourselves, "I'm too stressed out," "I'm too tired," "I'm too busy," "I'm too upset." We claim, "I don't have enough confidence or energy," "That's just the way I am," or "I can't do this on my own."

Here's the situation: You can pick any excuse. Each excuse works as well as any other. No matter what your reason is, you are using it to stop you from doing what you know you should be doing. You are allowing excuses to paralyze you.

Your excuses may be true and worthy, but it doesn't really matter. The fact is, if you want to improve your life, you need to figure out how to overcome these destructive self-messages.

Think of your "Top Three" favorite excuses for not saving. Write them down and take a look at them.

Use automatic savings

Automatic savings is an automatic deduction from your payroll check or your bank account. It puts a designated amount of money directly into your savings account weekly or monthly. You never even see the money. After you set it up, the process works in your favor. Studies show that they help savers stick with their savings plan.

Automatic savings takes only a few simple steps to set up. Some plans can fund investments that earn. Study the 401(k) plans and savings plans offered at your place of employment. Be sure that you understand your options thoroughly.

Use automatic deposit

You can have your paycheck automatically deposited. This way you can't misplace your paycheck, and your money is available to you faster than if you deposited it in the bank or credit union yourself. If you track your accounts online, you can see exactly what checks have been deducted and what haven't yet been cleared from your account. Don't forget to check your accounts frequently for errors.

Use automatic bill paying

Another technique is to pay bills automatically. This is when your bill payments are deducted from your account or payroll check and sent directly to the vendor to pay your bills. This prevents you from misplacing your bills, forgetting to pay them, or paying them late. If you've ever paid a bill late, you know about late fees and penalties. With automatic bill paying, your bills are paid on time, every time.

To make automatic bill paying work, be sure you have enough money in your account on the day that each bill payment transfer is put through. Otherwise, you will have overdraft charges or checks bouncing. You can protect yourself from overdraft fees by acquiring a line of credit linked to your savings account.

When you have several payments pending, many banks and credit unions now process the largest payment before they process the smaller payments. Why? As we mentioned in Chapter 4, they make money charging overdraft fees. They are more likely to collect those fees and more of them if they deduct the larger check before the smaller amount.

If you are concerned about exceeding your balance limit, put as much "padding" as you can into your account. But don't spend the padding!

Let others help you

You may be able to spread out the payments that are automatically deducted from your account. Ask your creditors to try to change the "due dates" on your bills so that they are not all due at the same time of the month. This will help you manage your finances and prevent any overdraft fees and late fees.

Also, the representatives of your local bank or credit union can be a good resource of advice and information. Go in, make an appointment, and create an alliance with them. You need good partnerships on your way to wealth. Ask for suggestions about how you can do a better job budgeting, saving, and eliminating fees. They are eager to help.

It's not the wishing;
it's the doing.

Chapter 8

BEWARE OF CREDIT CARD DEBT

"Money often costs too much."
—Ralph Waldo Emerson

Before the days of easy credit, people had to be patient and save until they could afford what they wanted. Patience was considered a virtue.

Now, many consumers have become victims of credit. They can get knocked out by credit's one-two punch: interest payments and fees that (1) add up in a short time, and (2) hang around for a long time.

Credit opportunities have turned consumers into credit slaves. "I'm not a slave to debt," you may tell yourself. "I pay my minimum payment on time every month." Unfortunately, if this is what you do, you will continue to bear a heavy burden.

How many times have you resolved to pay more than the minimum payment this month, but you ended up saying, "I'll wait and do it next month." Meanwhile, you waste today's income paying off the interest you acquired from yesterday's pleasure. The pleasure is in your past, but the burden is in your future.

Credit cards have enormous cost

Credit cards are costing you dearly. Here are some examples:

Example 1: Let's say you want to buy some new technology, a laptop computer, or a big screen television. You decide to incur a $3,000 debt on your credit card that charges you 19.8% interest. That's a high interest rate, but many credit card companies are raising interest rates.

If you pay only the minimum required monthly payment, it would take 39 years to pay off the $3,000! (That's assuming that you never mailed a payment late or incurred late fees, which would add to your balance.)

Why would it take 39 years to pay it off? The reason is that you would be paying more than $10,000 in interest. Here's the saddest part: You won't be using that laptop or big screen television after 39 years, even though you are still paying for it.

Example 2: Here's a slightly happier scenario. Say you bought something for $2,000 on a credit card that charges 18% interest. If you make only minimum monthly payments, it could take 30 years to pay the debt off.

In the meantime, you have generously paid your credit card company over time about $4,900 in interest. That means your $2,000 purchase wasn't such a bargain after all. It actually finally cost you $6,900!

Example 3: At this printing, the average household owes about $10,000 on credit cards at an annual rate of 15%. This costs about $1,500 a year in interest.

Say you invested that $1,500 instead of paying it out in interest every year. After 40 years at an 8% interest rate you would have an extra $181,700. That's an example of how you can make interest work for you instead of against you.

Some Credit Card Do's

Avoid paying interest and fees

"Low" monthly installment plans are designed to make you feel comfortable--and make your creditors rich. It's easy to convince yourself, "Somehow, I will be able to afford the minimum monthly payment." This is dangerous. Instead, make sure that the minimum payment is easy for you and that you will make much larger payments every month in order to avoid paying large amounts of interest.

If you can't pay the entire balance, at least pay more than the minimum payment required. Smaller payments now cost more later in deeper and longer debt. It just doesn't make sense to pay the minimum payment. Minimum payments add years and thousands of dollars in interest payments. That's because the interest keeps accruing—and the interest on the interest keeps accruing.

Credit cards also are designed to slowly consume your money by charging late-payment fees and over-the-limit fees. On some credit cards, if you pay just one day late, you could be charged a late fee. Plus, the credit card company also could increase your interest rate. Over-the-limit-fees can be charged to your account if you spend just one penny past your credit card limit.

Use a plan to eliminate your debt

Wipe your debt column clean. You can do this slowly, but firmly. Take portions of your outstanding debts and pay off a large chunk every month.

Here's how to get started: Make a master chart of your debts--who you owe, how much you owe, the minimum monthly payment, the interest rate, and the remaining payments. Add up all the minimum monthly payments.

This is your "monthly payment budget." This amount is the amount you are going to pay every month until all of your debts are paid off. First, pay off your credit card with the highest interest rate as soon as you can. When that card is paid off, more funds are freed up from your "monthly payment budget" to pay down more of the balance of the other credit cards and eliminate them faster. Keep paying the same amount toward your credit cards until all of the cards are paid off.

As we suggested earlier, consider using some of your savings to pay off credit cards with high interest. Then build your savings account back up and don't use your credit card after it's paid off. Plan a little reward for yourself when each card is paid off. Then start paying off the next card. When all the cards are paid off, celebrate—and don't use your credit cards except for true emergencies.

Get help if you need it

You may have more debt than you can handle by yourself. More drastic measures may be required, such as negotiation with your creditors for debt relief.

If you are having trouble making your monthly payments, here are some useful websites for credit card debt counseling:

- **www.consumerlaw.org**
- **www.creditguard.org**
- **www.familycredit.org**
  (free booklets on saving)
- **www.myfico.com** (free booklets and a free newsletter about how to save)
- **www.usoba.org** under the consumer link (government advice on choosing the best credit reduction strategy, free newsletter, and money saving tips)
- **www.ftc.gov/bcp/online/pubs/credit/repair.shtm** (government advice on choosing the best credit counselors)

You can also contact the National Foundation for Credit Counseling at **www.nfcc.org** (800-388-2227).

Pay your credit cards off in full every month

After you learn to control spending and reach your savings goals, you can start using credit cards carefully, charging only the amount that you can pay off fully each month. Surely, you've noticed how interest charges quickly and quietly devours your income. Now, you will never waste money on interest again.

How will you know what your balance will be each month on each card? Just keep a memo of the date, the amount, and the location of each purchase. That way, when the bills arrive, you will be prepared.

Don't take on more debt

Credit card companies are very aware of when you pay off a credit card. It affects their bottom line because now they won't be able to count on you giving them all those interest payments. They want you back into debt. Creditors may start offering you more credit or a higher spending limit, but don't fall for it!

Refuse these offers or you will be pulled down into out-of-control credit again. If they offer you a higher credit limit, refuse it. If they give you credit card checks, shred them. If they send you more credit cards, cut them up.

Report lost or stolen cards right away

Most credit card companies have toll-free numbers and 24-hour service to report lost or stolen credit cards. Keep a copy of the front and back of your credit cards at home, so that this information is readily available. Once you have reported the loss or theft of your card, you usually have no more responsibility for unauthorized charges beyond $50 per credit card.

Acquire credit cards carefully

Some credit card companies offer a "fixed" interest rate. But the "fixed" rate can change without notice. Check your statement every month to see if the interest rate has been increased. If so, call the credit card company to complain. The

Federal Reserve is trying to require credit card companies to commit to a specific time period before they can raise the "fixed" interest rate on their cards. However, at the time of publication, these efforts are on going.

Credit card "enhancements," such as travel discounts, gift certificates, and other offers are designed to lure you into obtaining and using credit cards. Face it, once you receive a new credit card, it's hard not to use it and dig yourself deeper in debt. Resist the temptation.

Buff up your credit rating

One missed payment can lower your credit rating by as much as 100 points. Overdraft charges affect your credit rating, too. As we said before, a poor credit rating can prevent you from buying a home, buying a car, or obtaining a loan. Banks and credit card companies offer lower interest rates to consumers with good credit ratings. A lower interest rate means you save when you need a loan. What is your credit rating as of today? One way to find out is to go to **www.myfico.com**.

Some Credit Card Don'ts

Don't keep more than two credit cards active

Have a Visa or MasterCard, since some merchants don't accept American Express. An American Express card may be useful if you travel frequently.

Make sure the credit cards you carry have the lowest interest rate available on the market. When possible, switch to a credit card with a lower interest rate. To comparison shop rates, go to **www.cardratings.com**, **www.creditrate.com** and **www.bankrate.com**.

If you have too many credit cards, pay off the extra cards, cut them up, and cancel them.

Don't forget to keep your eyes on the calendar.

You've heard about "no interest, no payments for a year" credit offers with major purchases. Beware that, at the end of that first year, the interest rate can jump to a very high rate. Unless you are extremely disciplined and pay the debt off early, these offers can cost you a large amount of money.

When you are offered "no interest" for a year, find out exactly when that year ends and make sure that you can pay off the entire balance long before that date. If you don't pay it all off early, you may have a heart attack when you see your new, higher interest rate.

Here is a strategy for those of you who have discipline. If you have the cash on hand for the purchase, ask if you can negotiate a discount for cash. If you can't negotiate a discount, you could take the "no interest" offer and make the purchase. Then take your cash on hand and invest it in an interest bearing account. Be sure to remember to pay off the debt before the "no interest" period ends.

Don't get into an anxiety habit

Debt creates stress, irritability, and anxiety. This can affect your health and your relationships. You may tell yourself that high levels of debt are "just a part of life." Nevertheless, trying to keep up a wealthy appearance for neighbors, family, and friends can eventually create a heavy burden. We urge you to end the charade. Face up to your feelings of inadequacy. Explore how much you value yourself. Know that the value of each person is so much more than their paycheck or their possessions.

Don't be afraid to ask for help

If you are having trouble controlling your spending, you may benefit from talking to others who have overcome the same problem. Debtors Anonymous **www.debtorsanonymous.org** uses the very successful 12-Step Program format. You can learn to refuse to use your credit card just as an alcoholic refuses to use alcohol. As in any 12-Step Program, you learn you can fight your demons "one day at a time."

Don't use your credit to pay for vices

Out-of-control gambling, smoking, drinking too much, and illegal drug use are vices that can create financial disaster. These weaknesses drain their victims personally and financially.

Gambling can cause financial strain and divorce. Smoking creates health problems that result in medical expenses and a shortened lifespan. Smokers also pay higher premiums on their life insurance, health insurance, auto insurance, and property insurance. Alcoholism can slowly destroy one's health, happiness, and family life. The most vicious of all personal demons, illegal drug use, is extremely expensive and potentially deadly.

You may know that these vices are bad for you. Even still, one or more of them may have a steel grip on your life and your finances. If so, do the most simple—but perhaps the most difficult—thing you will ever do: admit that you are addicted and that you can't stop by yourself. Then you will find out the good news that you are not alone and that help is available.

Help is available to reclaim your life, your health, and your finances. Click onto **www.nicotine-anonymous.org, www. gamblersanonymous.org, www.alcoholics-anonymous. org, www.na.org** (Narcotics Anonymous), **www.ca.org** (Cocaine Anonymous) and **www.addiction.recov.org** (Illinois Institute for Addiction Recovery). Also, ask your employer or church for referrals to support groups or counselors.

It's not the credit card that is the master;
you are the master.

Chapter 9

SAVING MONEY WITH A BUDGET

*"Save a part of your income and begin now,
for the man with a surplus controls circumstances
and the man without a surplus is controlled by circumstances."*
—Henry H. Buckley

In order to hang onto your money, you are going to need a budget. A budget helps you control your spending so it doesn't control you. A budget is simply a road map that lays out the amount of money you have coming in and gives you guidelines on how to spend it. Here are some suggestions how to make a budget and stick with it.

Great plans need action to be great

A budget is a plan that won't work unless it is put into action. Once your budget is in place, you can adjust it as needed. Only you know what you really need to include in your budget and what you can eliminate. Each budget is very personalized. If you design your budget for your specific needs and circumstances, you will gain control over your money.

"Most people don't plan to fail, they just fail to plan." Without a plan, your money will disappear and you won't know where it went. Make a plan to keep track of where your money goes throughout the day, the week, the year, and your entire life. This is the first key to financial success.

Use a budget guide

To set up your budget, you can use one of many budget guides available. There is a 27-page budget guide on **www.familycredit.org** which provides worksheets to list creditors and calculate your net worth, income, expenses, monthly budget, and bi-weekly budget.

At **www.teachmeaboutcredit.org** (800-994-3328), you will find a personal budget guide, as well as newsletters that will send you monthly budgeting tips. The Personal Credit Guide points out how you can save thousands of dollars simply by eliminating unnecessary purchases such as sodas, donuts, morning cappuccino, video rentals, and cigarettes. If you are in the habit of buying your lunch on workdays, you may be paying at least $6 per day. If you make your lunch at home and bring it to work, you would save $1,500 per year. Not only that, you could experience two other benefits: you could finish your work earlier and you could lose weight!

Be realistic

Everyone has more expenses than they think they have. When you design your budget, be honest with yourself. First add up all of your fixed monthly expenses. Then add in fixed annual expenses including the premiums on all of your insurance policies and property taxes. Make a rough estimate (on the high side) for what you usually pay for taxes, annual physicals, dental cleanings, and car maintenance. Figure out how much you spend each year on gifts, travel, and home improvement. Don't forget that everyone has unplanned expenses for car repairs, home repairs, dental work, and doctor's visits.

Watch your inflow versus outflow

Now, take a look at your income compared to your expenses. Are you spending beyond your means? If so, you can earn more, spend less, or both.

After you take a realistic look at your situation, set some reachable milestones. Make sure that these goals are realistic, specific, and based on your actual income and outflow of money. Otherwise, you won't stay motivated and reach your goals. Examples of attainable weekly savings goals are to buy one less cappuccino per week, take your lunch to work once a week, or rent a movie once a month.

Review your assets and debts on a regular basis. Update your budget periodically to stay motivated. Even millionaires need to manage their wealth with a budget--or they won't remain millionaires!

Understand different kinds of expenses

To master your finances with a budget you need to know about three kinds of expenses: fixed expenses, flexible expenses, and discretionary expenses.

Fixed monthly expenses: necessary items that stay the same every month. This category can include rent or mortgage payments; loan payments; transportation such as car payments or bus fares to get to your job; and health, car, and life insurance payments.

Flexible monthly expenses: necessary items that change every month. This category can include food, utilities, credit card payments, haircuts, necessary household items, necessary clothes, etc.

Discretionary expenses: non-necessary items. This category can include dining out, movie and concert tickets, entertainment, club dues, books, music, electronics, video games, sports, travel, gifts, hobbies, extra clothes, furniture, beverages, etc.

Discretionary items are bought with disposable income.

Know your disposable income

This is how to determine your disposable income each month:

First, when you get your paycheck, put money into your savings account, where you can't get your hands on it easily.

This is how you "pay yourself first." To pay yourself first is the cornerstone of your savings plan.

Second, set aside the money you need to provide for your fixed monthly expenses (see above).

Third, set aside the money you need to provide for your flexible monthly expenses (see above).

Fourth, set aside the money you need to pay your other bills.

Fifth, take a look at what you have remaining. This is called disposable income. This is what you might choose to spend on discretionary expenses (see above).

After you have determined your disposable income for each month, put it in a special envelope or special account to save for long-range discretionary expenses.

Remember to give yourself a small amount of spending allowance to use as you wish during the week. You need to give yourself this money every week even if it's only a few dollars. These few dollars will help prevent you from feeling so limited that you abandon your budget. This is your money to spend however you wish, without feeling guilty. Your spouse/significant other should be allotted the same amount of spending allowance to keep things fair.

Make your budget work

Here are some tricks to help make your budget work:

Take out the money for your savings account as soon as possible. Do the same for your fixed and flexible expenses. Otherwise, it's easy to spend it on other things!

As we have mentioned, your savings amount can be automatically deducted from your paycheck. Also, you may be able to set up online billing to pay certain fixed expenses directly from your paycheck.

For your fixed and flexible expenses, pay as many of them as you can in cash. Decide how much cash you can spend for each category each month. Make a list of your cash categories. Create a separate envelope for each category. Write the monthly amount for that category on the envelope. Each month, place the designated amount of cash into its designated envelope.

If you have cash left over in some of the envelopes at the end of the month, you can roll that cash over to the next month or put it in a special envelope.

Here's some advice on the psychology of budgeting: If your budget deprives you of too much too fast, you might give up. Instead, sneak up on yourself. Build in some buffer money at first. Make your budget realistic for where you are right now. Soon, you will find new ways to save and you will be able to save even more. But to start, make new changes gradually and add a few more changes over time.

Be patient, stick with it, and you will start to reach your goals, one at a time. When you do, you will be even more motivated, make more changes, and start to see results even faster!

Have goals

Have a long-term dream-goal to strive toward, even if at times you can only plod along slowly. Long-term goals help keep you from being frustrated by short-term obstacles. If you don't have a vision of a cherished financial goal—a car, a vacation, a home, comfortable retirement, college—you'll get bogged down in the day-to-day difficulties of life.

Remember the old sayings, "You can't hit a homerun unless you step up to the plate." "You can't catch a fish unless you put your line in the water." "You must be present to win." "If you shoot for the stars, at least you'll reach the moon." Choose a dream-goal that motivates you.

Now break your dream-goal into smaller steps. Can you become debt-free by the end of the year? Can you save a certain amount in six months? Can you pay off one credit card this month? What steps do you need to take this year, next year, and in the next five years? Make sure that your steps are doable and that you are willing to follow through with them, one at a time.

We believe that when you strive, you thrive.

Start with small changes

Start with small, easy behavior changes. You can make your own list, but here are few painless habits to get you headed in the right direction:

1. Keep a shopping list for every store you visit. Don't go to that store until your list is long enough. When you go to that store, bring your list and don't buy anything that is not on the list.
2. When you go to the grocery store, don't go when you're hungry. Eat a snack before you go. If you're hungry at the grocery store, you'll buy twice as much.
3. Try not to go to the grocery store with your children. If you must bring your children to the grocery store with you, give them a snack before you go. This avoids whining and extra purchases. Keep snacks in your car.
4. Try generic versions and store brands. You may be surprised to find that they are very similar to name brands. At the pharmacy, try the generic version of your drugs if your doctor allows it.

After you build one of these small changes into your life, adopt another change. Small steps will get you there. Just keep moving forward!

Make daily choices that matter

How you spend your money now determines how you will live in the future. Your choices either will lead to your dreams or destroy you. Choose actions that lead you toward your dreams, not away from them. Open your mind to opportunities to save more money and they will appear. Act on them and make them a part of your lifestyle.

Don't emphasize the temporary struggle necessary to achieve your dreams. Instead, focus on how wonderful it will be to achieve them. Of course, you will have moments of weakness; you will stray off course. The important thing is to get back on track as soon as possible. If you get stuck, whatever you do, don't go backward. Forgive yourself and move on.

Measure your progress through your daily choices. Be glad for even the smallest achievements. Reward yourself in small ways to keep yourself going. Plan a bigger reward for achieving larger milestone victories. But don't let your rewards put you back in debt again!

Use preparation and perspiration

Success requires both preparation (planning the work) and perspiration (working the plan). It's encouraging to know that if you prepare more, you'll perspire less! The same holds true for your savings and budgeting. A usable, well-designed budget creates a safety net for you. By preparing, you prevent unplanned perspiration.

Generation after generation, this advice is time-honored: First plan your work and then work your plan. One doesn't work without the other. A plan without work is just a plan. Work without a plan is just work.

Study up on it

Read books and magazine articles on how to save money. You can read many of these books and magazines free of charge at your local public library. See the Suggested Reading list at the back of this book for some reading suggestions.

Take advantage of free online magazines on personal finance. These publications often are available on the magazine racks at grocery stores and bookstores. But why buy them when you can get the information free online? If you don't have access to the Internet at home, you can use a computer at your library.

Here are a few magazine websites to visit:

- Good Housekeeping, **www.goodhousekeeping.com** (Click on the "saving money" tab, then the "budgeting and planning" tab)
- Better Homes & Gardens, **www.bhg.com** (inside the family and money section)
- CNN Money, **www.money.cnn.com**

- Real Simple, **www.realsimple.com**
- Consumer Reports, **www.consumerreports.org**

America Saves is a nationwide campaign of more than a thousand non-profit, government and corporate groups to encourage "financially vulnerable" people to save and build personal wealth. Even if you don't consider yourself "financially vulnerable," we suggest that you click on **www.americasaves. org** to find out more information and suggestions. Also, you can sign up for money-saving tips to be emailed to you daily at **www.dailycents.com**.

Television shows and television news segments offer financial advice and suggestions about consumer products. American Consumer TV **www.americanconsumer.tv** and Real Simple **www.pbs.org/realsimple** on your local public television station are two of many television programs you can watch.

Your newspaper may have a column on how to save. For example, the *Los Angeles Times* has a business section with savings tips. You can find out more at the *Los Angeles Time's* website: **www.latimes.com/costofliving**. Also, visit libraries and bookstores for books, audio tapes, and CDs with financial advice.

As with all advice, carefully analyze any financial advice that you hear or read about in the media. Remember, advice in the media is designed for the average person, not you specifically.

Ask for advice

When you meet people who are successful at keeping a budget, saving, and investing, ask them how they do it. You don't have to "re-invent the wheel."

Ask a qualified financial consultant about how you should save and invest your money. Examine their suggestions carefully and don't rush into anything. Ask lots of questions and listen to the consultant's answers. Do you understand their recommendations? You must decide if their advice is going to help you specifically, not "everyone else."

Even the best advice has its advantages and disadvantages. Sometimes in their eagerness to explain advantages of a particular product or strategy, consultants may neglect to fully explain the disadvantages.

One example of lack of explanation was the promotion of "sub-prime teaser-rate" home loans. These loans have a low "teaser" rate at the beginning, in order to help get the buyer into the loan. But the interest rate rises sharply when the loan rate "resets." Then the monthly house payment can skyrocket. When home buyers heard the advantages of these loans, they sounded like a great idea. They assumed that they would be able to handle the payments when they increased later. Many homeowners claim, however, that they didn't fully understand the potential disadvantages when they signed up for these loans.

As always, it's your responsibility to make sure that the source of any advice you consider—whether from the media, a friend, or consultant—is reputable and qualified to give advice on that topic. No one financial product or strategy is going to solve every financial problem. Test the advice against your "gut" instinct and your research. Does the advice help you reach your goals? (Or does it help the consultant reach his or her goals instead?) Consider carefully if the advice is practical for your specific circumstances and if you are truly comfortable with it.

Be prepared to adapt

"We've always done it this way." These six words are opportunity killers. Change is hard but sometimes it's necessary and often, it's good. Don't be afraid to try new approaches to see if they work for you.

The world will continue to change at an alarming rate, and your life will change along with it. Change is the only guarantee in life. It is the only thing we really can be sure of. We all have to live with the awareness that our current situation could change suddenly at any time—either for the better or for the worse. That is why we say, "Expect the best, but plan for the worst." Then you will be prepared for either situation.

Proactive people plan for any possibility. They are ready to adapt. You can be ready to adapt, too. Build your emergency savings fund now. Then you will be able to be flexible and adjust to changes in any economic environment.

Strengthen your character

The choices you make with your money show your true character. Are you competitive, greedy, or impatient? Are you unwilling to wait for what you want?

Take a look at yourself and your financial reality. Build your inner character by doing what you know is right with your finances. This is financial maturity: to accept responsibility for your financial reality and take actions to improve it.

It's not what you start with;
it's what you end with.

PART II

YOUR MONEY & OTHERS

Chapter 10

YOUR MONEY AND YOUR RELATIONSHIPS

*"Whoever originated the cliché that money is the root of all evil
knew hardly anything about the nature of evil
and very little about human beings."*
—Eric Hoffer

Money is not the root of all evil. In fact, money is simply a tool used to acquire products and services. Everyone uses money according to their own goals and motivations. How the money is used determines whether the money is "good" or "bad."

How do the people in your life spend their money? This is a very important question. If you share a residence with anyone—a spouse/significant other, a relative, or a roommate—he or she is your financial partner to some degree. He or she can help you or hurt you financially. Therefore, it's valuable to explore your financial partnership.

Who is your key financial partner?

If you are married, your spouse is your key financial partner. Even if you don't handle any of your spouse's money, you may still be responsible by law for financial decisions that your partner has made. Only a divorce would dissolve your legally binding partnership.

How well does your spouse/significant other handle money? Does he or she desire financial independence like you do? If not, you could be headed for serious, long-term problems both in your finances and in your relationship.

Decide who is the "spender" and the "saver"

Look closely at how your spouse/significant other handles his or her own money, as well as the money you share together. Both of you may say that you want to save money, but one of you may resent the other's desire to spend or may try to sabotage efforts to save.

The two basic approaches toward money are the attitude of the saver and the attitude of the spender. The saver desires financial security above comfort and pleasure. The spender craves comfort and pleasure more than financial security. Are you a saver or a spender? Which one is your spouse/significant other? Are you working with each other, or against each other?

Don't be afraid to talk about it

Sit down and tell each other why you are a spender or a saver. Explore how your desire to save or spend is part of your desire to nurture your relationship and care for each other.

Be honest and try to understand each other. Share your inner fears. Acknowledge that each of you is trying to take care of each other in your own way. Since you are joined in a financial partnership, you need to agree on your financial goals and how you can work together to achieve them.

Find common ground, compromise, and meet each other in the middle. There is no question that being responsible and successful with financial matters leads to better and more meaningful relationships. Healthy relationships have enough mutual respect and commitment to adjust to each other's needs and concerns. Talk it out peacefully and thoughtfully. This will help lower some of the emotional walls that you may have built between you.

Don't let money strain your relationships

Studies have shown that financial stress is the primary cause of divorce. Money is the issue that couples argue most about.

When you have a conflict with someone about money, multiple things are going on. You are in conflict with yourself, and in conflict with the other person. Try to hear the real meaning behind each other's words. Try to understand your motivations and fears. If you can "hear" the inner dialogue, you can resolve conflicts with less damage to the relationship.

Everyone is influenced by a combination of money-thinking factors. Some of those factors are your childhood experiences, your experiences in the adult world, and your own expectations about what your life should be like. Money-thinking factors can be broken down into several categories, according to the book, *If I Think about Money So Much, Why Can't I Figure It Out?* by Arlene Modica Matthews (see the Suggested Reading list at the end of this book).

Create money harmony in the home

Here are some suggestions that will prevent money issues from straining your relationship:

- Invest time in your relationship to show the other person that he or she is more important than money.
- Read this book together, chapter by chapter. Underline the steps that you both are willing to try.
- Put together a reasonable, realistic budget that you both are willing to follow.
- Resolve to decide together before either of you makes major purchases.
- Promise to be open and honest with each other about your money decisions.
- Try to not be judgmental and argumentative.

If you need more help establishing harmony in your relationships, consider talking with a skilled professional. A therapist or qualified financial consultant might be able to help you decide together how to improve your mutual financial situation.

Take a look at the people around you

People tend to act similar to the people around them. Look at the people around you and your spouse/significant other. Do your friends and co-workers spend their money foolishly? Or do they know how to save and create value in their lives? How does their behavior influence both of you?

Communicate about purchases

One way to establish money harmony is to stick to your agreed budget. Another way is to agree on major purchases. Your own definition of a "major" purchase depends on your income. For some couples, a "major" purchase is anything that costs more than $5. For other couples, a "major" purchase is anything that costs more than $500.

Don't make "major" purchases without your partner's approval. If your partner purchased something "behind your back" that you objected to, resist the temptation to retaliate by buying something you shouldn't buy. Remember, money taken from a joint account or joint credit card belongs to both of you.

If you are on a very tight budget for awhile, it helps if each of you has an equal amount of spending allowance for each week. Hold each other accountable for being committed to not spending more than that amount.

Some couples report they reduce arguments over money by designating their money as either "yours," "mine," or "ours." That means that they each have their own separate checking account and a joint checking account. They each have their own separate credit card and they share a credit card in both of their names. As an added benefit, this practice can help establish a positive credit rating for a stay-at-home spouse.

It's not what you spend together;
it's how you spend together.

Chapter 11

YOUR MONEY AND YOUR CHILDREN

*"Money won't make you happy
—but everybody wants to find out for themselves."*
—Zig Ziglar

The desire to save is in Sam's and Heidi's DNA—thanks to their parents. They didn't always enjoy learning the lessons their parents taught them, but they learned to appreciate those lessons. Give your children the same gift—the gift of knowing how to save.

Tell your children the truth about money

Children form their ideas about money very early. It's no wonder that they are confused about money. Children watch us when we use our credit cards and debit cards. They watch us when we get money from ATM windows. How can they understand the concept of earning money through employment? They don't see you put in the hours at the office and then receive your paycheck.

Children have to learn from experience--as we all did--where money really comes from. Money doesn't come from an ATM, a credit card, or a debit card. It comes from working, saving, and making good investments.

Don't hide your children from "the real world" of money. They need to understand the reason they can't have everything they want. It's the same reason you can't have everything you want! They need to know that you make mature decisions about your money. Don't be afraid to say to your children, "I would love to buy that for you. Unfortunately, it doesn't fit with my budget right now. If you really want it, you can save your own money and buy it yourself."

Give your children an allowance

Help your children understand that money needs to be earned, saved, and spent wisely. Start when they are young. Give them a small allowance before they start kindergarten. Let them make their own decisions about how to spend their allowance.

Give them a small wallet to hold their money when they go to the store. At the store, when they ask you to buy them something, tell them that they can use their own money. Help them count their money and determine if they can afford the item.

Help your children set savings goals, such as to save for a special gift or for souvenirs on your family vacation.

Set limits

To raise children requires more money than ever. The costs for childcare, schools, and college go up all the time. These are costs that you may not be able to control. But you can set limits on your children's spending. When your children grow older and they have a cell phone, limit the amount of money you will pay for their cell phone bill. Children should pay for extra cell phone charges with their own money. This encourages them to limit use of non-necessary services, such as text messaging, video games, and Internet access.

If you decide to give them a pre-paid credit card or a debit card, set limits. Offer to pre-pay the card with the same amount on the same day of each month--no exceptions.

Help them to help you

Every generation of parents has discovered the same thing: their children don't really appreciate their parents' sacrifices until they become parents themselves.

Nevertheless, when your children are old enough, they need to understand that they are part of a family and everyone has to pitch in. By the time they are teenagers, they should be helping to maintain the lawn, clean their bedrooms and bathrooms, wash their laundry, cook, and clean the dishes after mealtime.

Protect your children from temptation

We believe that prepaid credit cards for children generally are a bad idea. These cards train children to depend on credit cards. How much better to teach your children to be on a cash-and-carry basis and actually see their money enter and exit their wallet!

Share this book with your children as soon as they are old enough. Forewarn them about the dangers of debt, hidden costs, and fees. Seek out books and programs to teach your children how to be responsible with their money and become financially literate. Promote financial literacy education for children and teens in your community's schools.

Show your children it's fun to save

Here's an easy way to show your children how small savings can add up fast: Have everyone in your family toss their loose change into a big "savings jar" at the end of each day. In a few months when the jar is full, help your children take the jar to your bank or credit union. Some will count your change in a change-counting machine at no charge.

Let everyone in the family write down what they think the total amount of change will be. The person who comes closest to the total chooses the family activity on which the money will be spent. The family activity could be dining out or a day at an amusement park. Make sure the activity benefits the entire family, since everyone puts their change into the jar.

Sam notes that if you spend the family savings jar money on family outings, you are not putting the money away for long-term investment and growth. Heidi points out, however, that memories of family bonding times are important, too.

Make saving a part of everyday life

When your children are young, they can save some of their allowance in their piggy banks. Many parents require their children to save a certain portion of their allowance and money gifts.

When you take your children to the grocery store, show them how you comparison shop and use coupons to save money on food.

When they grow older, your children can open up a savings account at your bank or credit union and watch the balance grow. They can earn money by mowing lawns, babysitting, pet sitting, and organizing neighborhood garage sales. They can interview for summer jobs at stores or summer camps.

To give them incentive to work and put money away in their savings account, you may offer to "match" their funds or reward them when they reach a savings goal. This way, they can experience the satisfaction of selecting and buying expensive things they want and need, such as a computer, a car, or auto insurance.

Help them choose a college and a career

Make no mistake, the college your child chooses will directly affect both you and his or her financial situation in many ways for years to come. Find out the costs for tuition, room and board, and travel to the school. Does the school specialize in your child's desired career? Explain that career choices help determine lifetime income and standards of living.

To save on travel expenses, you and your child can "visit" many colleges remotely by viewing hour-long video tapes of college tours, available at **www.collegiatechoice.com**. Many college websites have online tours, also.

College costs increase every year. Students incur some of their deepest debts while in college. This is a heavy burden as they trudge out into the professional world after graduation. To help them control their expenses, set up a budget for them. Help them find a part-time job. Student loans take a long time to repay. Encourage them to apply for all available scholarships and grants.

You can get help with college tuition through the Federal Student Financial Aid Information Center **www.studentaid.ed.gov** (800-433-3243). If you have student loans, perhaps you can consolidate them. Visit **www.loanconsolidation.ed.gov.**

Be the role model they need

Our children are always watching us. We need to do our best to set a good example for them about how to manage money. While it's not always easy, it shows we really care. Good money management is a "priceless" gift that will benefit our children all their lives.

It's not how much you spend for your children;
it's how much you care for your children.

Chapter 12

GIFT GIVING AND YOUR RELATIONSHIPS

"Too many people spend money they haven't earned,
to buy things they don't want,
to impress people they don't like."
—Will Rogers

Gift giving is a big part of our culture. Sometimes, it can be stressful. You may feel insecure if you don't have the right gift for special occasions such as birthdays, showers, weddings, and holidays. You may be tempted to spend more than you should, particularly if the person you are buying the gift for is wealthier than you are.

The excellence of a gift lies in its appropriateness. Overly expensive gifts give a false impression and are motivated by insecurity. What you consider to be a generous gift should be generous compared to your income, not compared to the income of the receiver.

As in everything in life, you have to hang onto your self-respect and stay within your budget. Here are some ways to save money on gifts.

Give gifts for the right reasons

Keep your reasons for giving pure. Some people put themselves at financial risk when they give lavish gifts they can't afford. Why do they do this? They could be trying to "buy" acceptance, prestige, forgiveness, or love. If you are tempted to do this, take a look at these toxic motivations and what they are doing to your financial future.

Remember the classic Beatles song, "Can't Buy Me Love"? You may be tempted to overspend in an attempt to win someone's affection. Ask yourself some difficult questions: Is this gift really going to make a difference in your relationship? Are you being "used" or taken for granted? Are you giving a "making up/apology" gift instead of changing the behavior that made the apology necessary in the first place?

Give gifts that will be appreciated

A relationship can be damaged when one partner expects the other partner to "read their mind" and somehow know what they want. Most of us are not good mind readers. It helps if the other person tells you if they have a specific desire.

If you have to figure it out by yourself, be observant. Listen for mention of interests and hobbies. Ask subtle questions to get more information. Observe the things they already have. People who know each other well can give more obvious, specific hints.

Give gifts that make a difference

There is an old saying, "If you give someone a fish, you have fed him for a day. If you give someone a fishing pole, you have fed him for the rest of his life." Your gift can be the gift of mentoring, education, or training. Consider giving the gift of career education to those about whom you care.

A gift that can make a difference is a good book. The right book read at the right time can literally change someone's life. You can shop for and send a book easily and inexpensively at many bookstores and book websites.

Be practical. When giving gifts and presents, give something that is practical and that will help the recipient to reach financial independence. Gifts of cash, for those who need it, enable the receiver to use the gift most effectively. Ask your accountant about any federal or state gift taxes that you might have to pay as the result of giving a large gift of money.

Use windfalls carefully

A windfall puts you in a vulnerable position. Remember this whether you are the giver or the receiver. Windfalls and surplus cash include bonuses, commissions, inheritances, lottery or gambling winnings, prizes, dividends and earnings, and financial gifts in the form of cash, real estate, stocks, or bonds.

If you are fortunate and receive a windfall or surplus cash, don't use it foolishly. Use it only for investing long-term in assets that will grow in value, produce income, and increase your wealth. You can invest in yourself long-term by spending it on your education or career advancement. As we explain later, you need to invest in "cows" that give wealth, not "alligators" that consume wealth.

Don't treat the windfall or surplus cash as income and spend it. Instead, treat it as capital. Don't touch the capital, the gift itself. Use only the interest that the gift earns when it's invested wisely. This is an important opportunity that must not be wasted. We repeat: Do not spend your capital!

Carefully consider your *TheSmartestWay*™ "wants and needs" question: "What do I need (not want) to do with this money?"

Remember, this windfall or surplus cash may be subject to taxes. Consult with your tax preparer or accountant. Take the anticipated taxes off the top right away, and set the taxes aside in a separate account.

Give gifts that accomplish your highest goals

The famous story, "The Gift of the Magi" by O. Henry is about two young lovers at Christmastime. The young husband wants to give his wife the most wonderful gift he can afford, a gold comb for his wife's beautiful long hair. To earn the money, he sells his precious heirloom, the pocket watch that his grandfather had given him.

The wife wants to give her husband something very special, too. As fate would have it, she cuts off her hair and sells it to earn the money to buy her husband a chain for his pocket watch. The gifts that they give each other are now useless, since he no longer has his prized pocket watch and she no longer has her long hair.

It's a bittersweet, romantic story, but it's also tragic. To avoid such calamity in your own life, don't allow overpowering emotion to dominate your gift giving. Make sure that your gifts accomplish your highest goals.

Sam points out that the star-crossed lovers in the story would have been much better off if they had communicated with each other. In an ideal world, they would have combined their gift money into saving for a long-term goal such as their dream home, a second honeymoon, retirement, or education to help them qualify for a higher-paying job.

Gifts can be thoughtful and inexpensive

The value of a gift isn't how much money you spent on it. The fact that you went out of your way to be thoughtful is what matters most. Give of yourself. James Russell Lowell said, "Not what we give, but what we share…for the gift without the giver is bare." Instead of spending extra money, spend extra thoughtfulness. The best gifts are creative. Give something selected specifically to please.

Tasteful but inexpensive gifts can be found at stores such as Stein Mart **www.steinmart.com**, World Market **www. worldmarket.com**, and Nordstrom Rack **www.nordstrom. com**. You can find unusual and memorable gifts that are not expensive on **www.ebay.com** and **www.froogle.com**. Froogle is Google's product search site.

Gifts can be spontaneous

Heidi balances her passion for spontaneous gift-giving with her need to balance the family budget. When she is at stores such as 99 Cents Only Store **www.99only.com** and the Dollar Tree stores **www.dollartree.com**, she find little gifts and creative gift bags, wrapping paper, and tissue.

Whenever she needs a last-minute gift, Heidi usually can find the perfect item in her spare gift box. When her delighted friends and family ask her where she bought their gift, she usually can honestly reply, "I really don't remember!"

Give gifts you create yourself

Give of yourself personally by being very creative with the gift, even using your own personal skills to create it. Handmade gifts have so much meaning because you took the time and made the effort. Your creation doesn't have to be perfect. The little handmade cards and gifts children give their parents are treasured, though they are far from perfect. What counts is not the amount of money you spent on a gift, but your personal involvement.

For example, one of Heidi's most treasured gifts from her childhood is the handmade Valentine's Day card that her mother made from leftover fabric, ribbons, and buttons. Heidi enjoys scrap booking and making one-of-a-kind cards.

A gift can be carved, baked, built, painted, or pasted. You can paint or personalize a pottery item at a Color Me Mine store **www.colormemine.com** or create a one-of-a-kind necklace, bracelet, or earrings with a jewelry-making kit.

Give the gift of words

It's been said that "talk is cheap" and "actions speak louder than words." In many cases, this is true. Nevertheless, words that are a genuine statement of emotion can be rich with meaning—if they are the perfect words spoken at the perfect time and given with a perfect heart.

For example, we have a friend who fell in love with an attractive woman who dated men who gave her expensive gifts. The friend won her heart by being attentive to her emotional needs. The poems he wrote for her expressing his love were more treasured and effective in binding them together than any of the material gifts he could have given her.

We've all heard the bitter, sorrowful stories of people who would have done almost anything to receive the gift of the words "I love you." While words don't cost a dime, sometimes they are the hardest gift to give. If you need to give someone a few special words--whether it's telling your affection, appreciation, or even an apology--you may have to sacrifice some of your pride or resentment. But it's worth the price in order to give a gift that may be treasured for a lifetime.

Give the gift of time

The gift of your time is the most valuable gift of all. Your encouragement, humor, and affection are priceless treasures that will be remembered long after material gifts fade away. If you ever doubt this, just ask the child with a room full of toys but parents with no time to spend with them, or the wife with a luxurious home but a husband who is often traveling.

"I don't want more toys—I just want you to play with me," says the child. "I don't want more things—I just want you to be with me," says the wife.

For a truly memorable gift, give the gift of making a memory by spending time together. Plan an excursion that has sentimental significance. Plan a surprise that recreates a special moment or recalls an inside joke you shared together. A gift of a memory that you create by sharing your time, instead of your money, is beyond measure.

Give gifts that don't have issues

Give gift cards only when you know that the receivers really would appreciate it. Otherwise, you may always wonder if they ever even used the card. Gift cards can be redeemed only at a particular store, so they are not as practical as cash. (That store, by the way, has been enjoying the use of your money ever since you bought the gift card.)

Gift cards benefit stores in several ways. When you use the card, you may be very disciplined and buy something for less than the value of the card. The card, with the remaining balance, goes back in your wallet, where it continues to remind you to shop at that store again. By the time you return to the store, you may have forgotten the amount remaining on the card and end up spending more than that amount.

On the other hand, you may go to the store and buy something at a higher price than the value of the card. In either scenario, the gift card encouraged you to spend more than the amount on the card. That's the whole idea. Stores know this and they love it. Why do you think gift cards are sold everywhere?

Another problem with gift cards is that some are designed to become worthless over time. A number of years ago, Heidi learned this the hard way at a major discount store (there's one in every town across the land). After she discovered a gift card buried in her desk drawer, she went to the store to redeem it. When she made her purchase at the checkout counter, however, she was told that the card had zero value.

The manager made some calls to find out why. He was told that on the back of the card was an explanation about a "monthly non-use fee." This fee had devoured the entire value of the gift card. Heidi's two sons, who were young at the time, were with her. They were embarrassed that their mom was indignant about this store policy. But they also learned that it's appropriate to complain about unfairness.

Stay rational

Be cautious about life events that involve deep emotions, such as weddings. Don't let these events become a source of friction and anxiety. Don't let them delay your goal of financial independence because you feel pressured to spend beyond your means.

The Broadway musical entitled A Catered Affair by Harvey Fierstein shows the humor of this kind of situation. Set in the Bronx in 1953, the story is about a couple's dilemma of whether to invest their life savings in a business or spend it all on their only daughter's catered wedding.

It's easy to overspend on weddings and wedding gifts, but it's not necessary to do so. For example, Heidi's most cherished possession is the wedding ring given to her by her husband Bill. The total cost was $300 because the ring's "gem" is a glowing pearl. But the symbolism is priceless for her and she beams when she receives compliments on it.

Keep your sanity during the holidays

Don't wait until the last minute to shop for holiday gifts. Heidi buys a few gifts each month throughout the year when she finds them on sale. That way, she doesn't suffer from "post-holiday financial shock." She wraps and labels the gifts. She goes to the post office after Thanksgiving and avoids long lines and "rush" shipping charges. Then she relaxes and enjoys the true spirit of the holidays.

Sam knows of large families that "draw names" at holiday time. This practice allows you to give one expensive gift to the name you drew. You, in turn, get one expensive gift from the person who drew your name. Usually there is a maximum price that you are allowed to spend on the gift. Some prefer this instead of buying gifts for every family member. This avoids embarrassment for those who cannot afford gifts for everyone.

Start a holiday fund that you put spare money into each month. At the beginning of the year, calculate your annual gift fund total. For example, if you want to spend $1,200 per year on gifts, save $100 each month. Keep track of what you spend on gifts, so you don't deplete your fund before the year is over.

It's not how much you spend on a gift; it's what you give and how you give it.

PART III

YOUR MONEY & THE WORLD

Chapter 13

WHAT'S BEHIND YOUR OVER-SPENDING

"You must be in control.
Capital can do nothing without brains to direct it."
—J. Ogden Armour

Before you can control your spending, you need to know why you spend. If you are feeling insecure, you may go shopping to find something that will help you feel more attractive or more valuable. Sometimes when people are anxious about money, they do the opposite of what they know they should do: they go out and spend even more money.

If you have this problem, you need to start "rewiring" your spending habits. Here are some suggestions.

Don't purchase items you cannot afford

You know in your heart if you really can afford something. You know if a purchase is going to keep you awake worrying at night. Instead, plan for long-term rewards. If you are careful now, eventually you will be able to afford anything you want.

The competitiveness in our materialistic society causes us to make financial decisions that are not in our best interest. With whom are you competing--and why? Does that person have a higher income than you? If so, the playing field isn't level, and you have to keep that fact in mind.

Don't forget the tortoise and the hare

The story of The Tortoise and the Hare is about competitiveness and pride. The hare, a jack rabbit, was prideful, and teased a turtle until he agreed to race him. The turtle was slow and steady, but he never stopped. The rabbit was overly confident, so during the race, he decided to take a nap. You can guess who won.

Sam knows of two brothers. The first one started out with an annual income of about $125,000 per year, and the second one earned $500,000 a year. The one with the lesser income lived comfortably but modestly and traveled on vacations locally. The one with the larger income spent lavishly and toured the world.

After forty-five years in their respective careers, which brother ended up a multi-millionaire? The one with the smaller income. He didn't overspend on anything that didn't have long-term value. Instead, he invested all he could and made the magic of compound interest work for him. The other brother, although his income was four times greater, now has only 10% of the first brother's net worth.

Don't be afraid to develop a "reputation"

So what if people think you're "cheap" or "tight with money"? That's okay. To be a good saver, you can't be concerned about what other people think or say about you. They need to know that you don't want to waste your money and that you don't want them to waste your money, either.

Your thrifty nature may even make you a legend. Take Sam's "Toothpaste Story." Years ago, Sam hired a new attorney who sometimes seemed overly impressed with the large sums of money necessary to complete their real estate deals. During a high-powered meeting out of town, Sam put a $1,000,000 cashier's check on the table. The meeting took longer than anticipated, so Sam and the attorney had to find a hotel and stay overnight. They stopped at the hotel's gift shop to buy a few toiletries for their overnight stay.

The attorney stood in line at the checkout counter with a hair brush, toothbrush, and toothpaste. Sam was standing in line with a comb, toothbrush, and toothpaste. Sam told the attorney, "All you need is the toothbrush and a comb, which costs 10% of the price of that hair brush. You can come over to my room and use my toothpaste."

Fifteen years later, the lawyer recounted the incident at a banquet celebrating his success. Apparently, Sam's comment had made a lasting impression on him!

Don't be pressured into lending money

Speaking of social pressure or "peer pressure," here's more good advice: Don't be pressured into lending money. Lending money can ruin your relationships. It happens all the time. Yet, sometimes the pressure is so great that you may be tempted to "give in" and "give a hand-out." We advise you: lend money only if you are willing to turn the loan into a gift.

Remember the rule to "put your own oxygen mask on first"? When you are asked to lend money remember this principle. You will be able to help others more in the future if you take better care of yourselve in the present. Fewer than half the loans to family and friends are paid back. Is it okay if you don't get the money back? Are you willing to make your loan into a "gift"? If not, don't give it. To reduce strain on the relationship, make the loan into a gift. Tell the receiver that he or she can pay it back when they are in a position to do so.

You may be asked to help someone by co-signing on a loan. The danger is that if the loan isn't paid off, you are responsible for the balance, whatever it may be. Also, your credit is damaged if the payments are late or in default. If the person were able to handle the loan himself, he wouldn't need you to co-sign the loan. Think about this carefully before you take on the liability of co-signing a loan.

Don't become addicted to Internet shopping

You can become addicted to shopping. First you start to crave the emotional "lift" that buying something gives you. Then you come down off that high and feel low because of the guilt and anxiety of spending too much. The cycle continues until it the emotions of highs and lows become difficult to control.

For the same reason, Internet shopping can become addictive. You may only "window shop" online to collect information and compare prices. Be watchful, however, that you don't become a frequent shopper on a many websites.

Of course, bargains can be found on many websites, including **www.ebay.com, www.overstock.com** and **www. craigslist.org**. Also, websites entice frequent visits by offering coupons, discounts, tie-ins, and interactive information.

Nevertheless, surfing the web can become habit forming, and your online purchases can add up quickly. No matter how or where you are spending, don't overspend.

Remember that time is money, too. Watch the amount of time you spend online. Your online time might be better spent on training that would help you get a raise in salary or on writing a book that would help you promote your professional reputation.

Don't buy for instant gratification

Instant gratification is getting something now rather than waiting. Resist cravings for instant gratification when shopping. Wait for the right time, when it fits your finances.

You may be tempted to buy things to comfort yourself or reward yourself. Nevertheless, the pain of debt lasts much longer than the brief pleasure of getting what you want immediately. Also, if you wait for something you really want, you appreciate it even more.

Charlie Chaplin once said, "The saddest thing I can imagine is to get used to luxury." Don't buy yourself everything you want when you want it. Instead, whenever the desire strikes you to buy things you don't need, look at where that money would come from. Set aside that money for paying off your debts instead. This will help you achieve financial independence, which has far greater value than instant gratification.

Don't confuse your priorities

Far more long-term satisfaction can be gained from personal relationships than from purchases. Do you love people and use things? Or do you love things and use people? This is a serious question.

For greater happiness in life, learn to resist the temptations of envy, pride, and greed.

Envy makes you unhappy because you are coveting other people's possessions. As Francis Bacon said, "The covetous man cannot so properly be said to possess wealth as that wealth may be said to possess him." We all know people who have more things than we have. Don't wish to have what they have. Instead, be glad for their success, and learn from them so you can be successful, too.

Pride is feeling superior to others when you earn a higher income or you have more possessions than someone else. But the world is full of people who have less than you do, so that's nothing to be boastful about. Unfortunately, grief often comes to those who put their financial goals ahead of their relationships. Remember the phrase, "Pride cometh before a fall."

Greed is a powerful temptation in our culture. Fortunately, most of us could survive just fine with much less. Think about how much you consume every day. The green movement is trying to conserve the earth's diminishing resources. For another perspective on how much we really need in order to be happy, check out the website **www.buylesscrap.com**.

Don't confuse your money with self-worth

You are not your paycheck. Your paycheck does not define your worth. Your spouse's/significant other's paycheck doesn't define your worth or their worth either.

Do not make purchases to help bolster low self-esteem. When money is used as a self-image prop, it leads to financial trouble, which then leads to more negative self-talk. Does a voice inside your head tell you that you don't deserve to be happy and financially successful? Refuse to listen, no matter who is saying it.

Money can't buy everything. One thing it can't buy is control. Money cannot control all circumstances and it cannot control all people, at least not in the long run. Don't use money to try to punish others by withholding money or by favoring one person over the other.

Here are some of the aspects of a good life that money cannot buy: health, longevity, happiness, and high self-esteem. Only training and experience can help you gain intelligence, good manners, good character, and good taste. It takes real effort to earn love, loyalty, respect, and friendship.

To have a good life and high self-esteem, use your money-- don't let it use you.

**It's not what you own;
it's who you are.**

Chapter 14

SAVING TIPS FOR FOOD AND TRANSPORTATION

"Beware of small expenses;
a small leak will sink a great ship."
—Benjamin Franklin

Saving will soon become an everyday habit for you. With daily practice, soon you'll start getting financially fit. Here are some more ways to save money.

Save on Food

Use coupons

Carve some of the fat from your food budget with coupons. It is estimated that many people save $20 to $30 per week on their groceries by using coupons. That adds up to about $1,000 per year! The time it takes for you to clip coupons is worth it, because it's tax free savings. You can find coupons at **www. dealtech.com**, **www.kroger.com**, **www.couponorganizer. com**, **www.keycodecoupons.com**, and **www.couponcabin. com**. Magazine websites such as **www.goodhousekeeping. com** and the Thursday and Sunday editions of the major and local daily newspapers also offer coupons.

Get into the habit of looking for coupons, cutting them out, and categorizing them. Keep in mind the concept of "wants versus needs" when using coupons. Just because you have a coupon for something doesn't mean you need to use it. Keep all of your coupons and gift cards in a special envelope. Keep the envelope in your car so it is always handy when you shop. Go through the envelope occasionally and toss out the coupons and gift cards that have expired.

Eat better, but eat less

Junk food isn't really food. It is full of "empty" calories that don't nourish your body. You will be surprised how much your grocery budget will shrink if you buy more healthy food and less junk food.

Spend your food dollars on organic dairy products, free-range chicken, and meat without hormones. It tastes better and you'll feel better. Good food also is more satisfying. Not only will your grocery budget slim down, your waistline will, also. What's not to like about that?

Avoid fast-food restaurants

Many fast-food restaurants are about the "fast" and not about the "food." Some fast foods are loaded with sodium (salt). If you are addicted to the fast-food habit, break it.

Keep handy, healthy snacks in your car or purse. Examples of these snacks are small bags of mini-carrots, almonds, popcorn, baked crackers, and low-fat mozzarella string cheese. These foods taste good with "eat-on-the-run" fruits such as grapes, apples, and bananas.

Make time in your life to eat at home instead of driving through a fast-food establishment. You can cook a simple, nourishing meal in about the same time that you can wait in a fast-food line. For example, you can buy a pre-roasted whole chicken or packages of pre-cooked chicken pieces to use in salads, burritos, or stews. Put a potato, sweet potato, or healthy microwave dinner in the microwave. You can prepare dinner the night before in a crock pot.

Rethink the "need" for sodas and coffee

Dependence on coffee and sodas is a touchy topic. Many people believe they can't function without their favorite beverage. It's almost an addiction. Unfortunately, most of these drinks are just water mixed with sugar or sugar substitute, chemicals, carbonation, caffeine, milk, or unhealthy milk substitutes, and flavoring. These drinks may taste good, but the bad news is that they drain your wallet and pad your waistline.

Liberate yourself from this dependency and learn how to function without these drinks. You may experience a slight headache or feel irritable as your body adjusts to the withdrawal from a mild addiction. If so, cut back gradually, but do cut back. You will improve your health and wealth at the same time.

Save on Transportation

Save on gas

The price of gas these days has captured everyone's attention. But you can find gas stations that have lower prices, sometimes 20 to 30 cents a gallon less. To make it worthwhile, fill up whenever you pass a station with a lower price.

Sam checks out the prices at the gas stations along his commute to his office, approximately five miles. There is a 10¢ to 40¢ difference in the price for the same grade of gas, depending on the location of the station and the brand of gasoline. If you fill your tank every two weeks, this can amount to several hundred dollars in savings per year.

Here are some ways to save on gas:

1. Comparison shop. Search for websites with local information.

2. Drive at an even pace. Avoid fast starts and sharp braking.

3. Use cruise control wherever appropriate to keep your pace even.

4. Combine your errands so you can do most of them in one trip or in one location.

5. Drive a fuel-efficient car.

6. If you choose a larger car for safety, choose one that is fuel efficient.

7. Walk or ride a bike for short trips.

8. Telecommute as often as you can.

9. Try to get flex-time with your job so that you commute during non-peak hours.

10. Remove unnecessary items from your trunk.

11. Keep your car in good condition and tuned up. Change the oil and keep your tires properly inflated, according to your owner's manual.

12. Use light rail, buses, and other forms of public transportation. They can be more convenient than you expect.

13. Car pool or van pool to work. Ask your employer to help.

14. Find out if your city provides subsidies for car pooling or van pooling.

15. Coordinate car pools for your children to go to school and set up schedules with other parents for after-school events.

16. If you have two cars, use the car that is more fuel efficient for daily commuting to school, work, and longer distances.

17. Sometimes, renting a car for long trips makes sense. That way, you can avoid extra wear-and-tear on your car and perhaps rent a more fuel-efficient car. Check out discount coupons at rental car websites such as Enterprise Rent-a-Car **www.enterprise.com**.

18. Drive within the speed limit. Driving at higher speeds uses more gasoline.

19. Use the right grade of gas. Check the owner's manual.

20. If you are frustrated by traffic jams, don't try to pass slow cars. Chill out and get some CDs or audio tapes to listen to in the car. Thousands of books-on-tape are available from audio book rental clubs on dozens of different topics. Take a look at the selection at **www. onthegobooks.com**, **www.simplyaudiobooks. com**, or **www.audible.com**. Motivational tapes, learning-a-language tapes, and MP3 downloads of trainings are other options. Also, you can rent audio books for free from your library.

Find the right car

The media tells us that driving the "right" car elevates us to higher status. Here's a story about someone who chose the wrong car.

Sam recently was invited out for dinner by an acquaintance. He knew that the man was having trouble meeting a monthly office rental of $600 per month. The man was looking for capital to back his real estate projects but never seemed to have money of his own to invest, even though he earned large commission checks.

To Sam's surprise, the man drove up to Sam's house driving a $85,000 Mercedes. This explained the problem. He was spending too much of his spare funds on a status car, even though he didn't need a status car to impress his clients. A $25,000 car would have been adequate for his needs.

Sam calculated that the difference between buying an $85,000 car and a $25,000 car would have given him $60,000 extra capital to help him develop his projects. Furthermore, investors like Sam tend to be more generous to those who have the discipline to build their cash reserves and thus build their credibility.

Pay cash

Next to your home, your car may be your second-largest purchase. Therefore, you need to buy your car carefully.

The least expensive way to buy a car is with cash, meaning no loan. Bear in mind that car dealers make money when they help you finance a loan. Therefore, you may get a better deal on a car if you don't tell the dealer you intend to pay with cash. When the dealer asks you how you are going to buy the car, simply say, "I'm not sure yet."

Whenever you receive an offer from a dealer, tell him you need to think about it. Give him your phone number and then walk off the lot. Often, he will phone you with an even better offer. He knows he has to compete for your business.

If you don't think you can afford to pay cash for your car, look for a car you can pay cash for. Heidi and her husband bought their Honda Civic with cash. It's a terrific car with high style and low gas mileage. Sam buys his cars with cash, also.

Remember Sam's first car story

Sam bought his first car with cash. In 1950, after his first year at Stanford University, Sam took a job as a children's overnight summer camp director in northern Canada. He and two other camp counselors decided they wanted to go to the nearest town on their days off to get a break from the young campers. The problem was that they needed transportation. So they each pitched in $50 and bought a 1936 Dodge sedan for $150.

It was no surprise that the car's brakes soon wore out. But the young men couldn't afford new brakes. Instead, they discovered that they could stop the car by putting it into second gear and coasting to a stop! At the end of the summer, they left the car at the camp. Sam wonders if it's still there. Now, when he fills his gas tank, he can honestly say that it costs him more than what he paid for his first car.

Do your homework

If you do your research, you will find a car you can afford and fits your needs. There are dozens of manufacturers, models, and dealerships from which to choose.

Adopt *TheSmartestWay™* philosophy and look at the big picture. Ask yourself: What kind of car and size of car do I really need? What can I really afford? How much will my auto insurance premiums increase? What am I willing to give up in order to afford the car?

Now, do your homework. The Internet is a good place to start. Search online at **www.kbb.com** (The Official Kelly Blue Book), **www.autosite.com**, **www.carfax.com**, **www. carwizard.com**, **www.consumerreports.com**.

In your research, look at gas mileage. If your car gets lousy gas mileage, that adds to the overall, long-term price of the car. To compute your total cost each month for your car, don't look only at the monthly payment and interest cost (if you have to finance it). Also add in the average monthly cost of gas, insurance, repairs, and maintenance. Remember that a more economical car will save you significantly on insurance, repairs, and maintenance.

Low gas mileage is a top priority. You can find hybrid cars that use less gasoline at **www.allhybridvehicles.info**. Look at hybrid versions of Honda Civic, Accord, Chevy Malibu, Prius, Camry, Highlander, as well as cars by Lexus, Nissan, and Saturn. With the price of gas these days, hybrids aren't just for environmentalists anymore.

Comparison shop

Once you have decided what types, brands, models, and years of cars you want to consider, start comparison shopping.

Whatever car you decide to buy, first compare the online prices to the dealer prices. The sticker price on the window is the highest price that the manufacturer recommends. You want to pay much less. Prices will vary from dealership to dealership. So will customer service.

Buy your cars like Sam buys cars

Don't hesitate to use one dealer against the other. They are used to it. They expect it. They just hope that you will decide to finally make your purchase with them.

When Sam bought a car recently, the local dealer quoted him a price that Sam thought was too high. Sam comparison shopped at another dealership that had the largest inventory of that make in the state. The second dealer was located some distance away, but the trip was worth it because he offered Sam a much better price.

Sam showed his local dealer the second dealer's price, and his local dealer matched it. The reason Sam wanted to finally buy from the local dealer was convenience. He knew he would get better service and more privileges wherever he bought the car, so he wanted to be local. Once again, it pays to comparison shop and use one price against the other.

Know the dealer's cost

When buying a car, Sam always determines the dealer's actual cost on all the accessories and add-ons. Accessories can include floor mats, chrome strips, specialty hub caps, GPS systems, and a myriad of other accessories. The price of some accessories can include as much as 40% in dealer profit. You can determine the actual cost from the American Automobile Association (AAA) **www.aaa.com**, the Official Kelly Blue Book **www.kbb.com**, and Edmund's **www.edmunds.com**.

Negotiate to have the accessories added to the car at cost, at the time of purchase. This can save quite a bit of money. Also, some accessories can be acquired at no cost when you negotiate the price, since the expense to the dealer may be minimal.

Find tips and quotes from websites such as **www.autobytel. com**, **www.autoweb.com**, **www.intellichoice.com**, **www. carpoint.com**, **www.carbargains.com**, and **www.carmax. com**. Check out **www.dontgettakeneverytime.com** and **www.nhtsa.dot.gov/cars/problems** (the National Highway Traffic Safety Administration).

Avoid the leasing trap

It seldom makes financial sense to lease a car, because leasing is the most expensive way to buy a car. It has been said, "Leasing a car is a poor man's way to look rich." Nevertheless, friends and car dealers may pressure you to lease. Almost half of all car purchases these days are leases. The dealers are happy about this, of course, because they benefit from handling the financing.

If you lease a car, you must make a down payment and monthly payments. These payments are lower than if you were buying the car. The longer the lease, the lower your monthly payment, but the higher the interest rate. Not only will you pay enormous interest payments during the lease, you may get hit with extra charges at the end of the lease, too.

As in renting an apartment versus owning a home, it's usually better to own than to rent (lease). Why? Because whoever owns the property--the home or the car--has control. For example, if you want to buy the car at the end of the lease period, you have to pay the dealer's price, even if the car has lost much of its value.

If you return the leased car instead of purchasing it, the dealer can require you to return the car in the same condition as when you bought it, minus "normal wear-and-tear." You must pay whatever the dealer charges you to fix anything. Also, if you had exceeded the mileage limit, you pay penalty fees.

If you choose to pay off your lease early, you may have to pay an "early termination" penalty. Lenders usually require this penalty because you are denying them the interest fees they were expecting to receive from you.

In addition, lease contracts are very difficult to understand. Make sure the dealer explains everything to you clearly, in detail and in writing. Print out all explanations of the policy. Remember, dealers have to compete, so almost everything is negotiable. So negotiate the best deal you can get.

Be careful with installment plans

If you can't pay with cash, you'll have to get a loan. When you are on the dealer's lot or in the showroom, you will be approached by convincing, enthusiastic salespeople. Before you know it, you'll be looking at attractive cars that are beyond your budget.

An installment plan offer may seem like "free money" that seduces you into buying a more expensive car. But beware: an installment plan costs you enormously in interest payments. That's why you need to first compare the dealer's loan offer with your bank's or credit union's loan offer. If possible, get a pre-approved loan from your credit union or bank before you go car shopping.

Make the largest down payment you can afford. Don't choose the longest payment plan, even though that lowers your monthly minimum payment. Remember, the longer you spend paying the loan back, the more interest you pay. Ask the dealer to calculate what the interest will be on the various payment options. You'll be surprised how fast the interest adds up. Longer payment plans often carry higher interest rates, too.

In an economic downturn, your installment payment may be harder for you to pay. Worst case scenario, the dealer could repossess your car. To lose your car through repossession is a major blow to your pride, your mobility, and lifestyle. It also inflicts permanent trauma to your credit rating. Before you purchase, bear in mind that if you pay in cash, your car cannot be repossessed.

Don't go "upside down"

You are "upside down" on a possession if you owe more in payments than the item is now worth. Here's how to find out if you are "upside down" on your car payment: Determine what you still owe on your car, including interest that you will pay. Then determine approximately what you could sell your car for today. Which is the higher number? Do you owe more than your car is worth? If so, you are "upside down" on your car ownership.

Buy a used car and buy it with cash

A new car goes down in value, depreciates, by 20% to 40% the minute you drive it off the dealer's lot. Just 20% of $20,000 is $4,000. We ask you, is a couple weeks of "new car smell" really worth $4,000?

The best car to buy is a used car. The best way to buy a car is with cash. Heidi's parents bought used cars with cash. That's how she and her husband buy their cars. Even Sam buys used cars when he feels it makes sense. He always pays cash.

Good quality, certified, pre-owned cars are available. If you shop carefully, you can find a well-maintained used car for half what a new one would cost. Before you buy a car, be sure to get the car's vehicle identification number (VIN). Click on **www. carfax.com** and type in the VIN. You will receive a vehicle history report of the car, including any accidents or flood damage the car may have suffered.

If you drive your car for a long time and get the full value from the car, eventually it may have very little resale value. You may want to sell it back to a dealer or trade it in. Before you decide what to do to get rid of your car, check with several dealers, as their offers will vary. If the car is valued at less than $500, you might benefit from a tax deduction by donating the car to a non-profit organization.

It's not what you drive;
it's what you pay for what you drive.

Chapter 15

SAVING TIPS FOR UTILITIES AND MEDICAL NEEDS

"Money isn't everything
—but it ranks right up there with oxygen."
—Rita Davenport

U tilities and medical needs take up more and more of our income. The cost for these necessities are increasing. Be a watchful consumer and you'll save money.

Save on Utilities

Lower utility bills

Insulate your home to prevent hot and cool air from entering your home. Lower your thermostat in the colder months when you are away or sleeping. Raise your thermostat in the warmer months. Ask your gas and electric provider for a free "energy survey" inspection to show you how to lower your energy bills. They may provide an optional "budget billing" to balance out your gas or electric bills. Reduce water use with fewer baths, shorter showers, and more efficient use of your dishwasher and washing machine. If your gas bill or water bill rises unexpectedly, check to see if your gas line or water pipe is broken or leaking. For TV service, buy the basic plan for your cable channels.

Save on phone bills

For long-distance phone calls, you can save by using discount phone cards from discount stores such as Wal-Mart (**www. walmart.com**) and 99 Cents Only stores **www.99only.com**.

Heidi has used one long-distance prefix code for years. It bills all domestic long-distance calls at five cents per minute. She dials the code number 1010811 before she dials the number she's calling. To try it out, dial that code number before the long-distance number you are calling. Note the length of the call. Then check your phone bill for the charge.

You can even switch from making nationwide calls from traditional phone service to Internet phone service. If you have a computer and you can be connected to the Internet continually, this may be a way to save money. The cost of new technology drops continually. Seek out the best deals.

Save on cell phone bills

Cell phone contracts can be tricky. Be sure to ask lots of questions and read the fine print for upgrade fees and cancellation fees. Comparison shop with all available carriers and ask each carrier why you should pick them instead of their competitors. When you get your bill, inspect it for inaccurate charges, services you didn't request, fees you don't understand, and penalties for exceeding allotted minutes.

Ask your cell phone carrier to analyze your calling patterns to see if you can switch to a less expensive plan

Beware of cell phone insurance policies. The replacement cell phone you receive through the insurance coverage may be used or refurbished.

If you use your cell phone frequently, you may consider canceling your landline phone in your home. But be sure to watch your charges and fees on your cell phone, especially when you are out of town. Roaming charges can be very costly.

If you need to be released from your cell phone contract, you may be able to find someone to take it over for you on websites such as **www.cellswapper.com** and **www.celltradeusa.**

com. Also, you may be able to get out of your contract if there has been a price change affecting your plan.

Complain effectively as a consumer

Whenever you have a complaint about a service or a product, first prepare your case. Write down the facts of your complaint. What went wrong? What did you try to do about the problem? What can the company do to resolve your complaint?

When you talk to a company representative, make a note of the date, the time, and the person's name, title, and phone number. Write down what the representative said and repeat it back to him or her to make sure you got it right. Then ask to talk to the supervisor.

Be friendly but firm. If you get a "no," ask to talk to the next person in charge. Keep going up the chain of command until you get an answer you can accept.

Customer service departments may not resolve your complaint promptly. You may become frustrated and give up. We've all heard the phrase, "the squeaky wheel gets the grease." It's true. Persistence helps.

If all your efforts bring no resolution, contact **www. consumeraction.gov** or your local Better Business Bureau office. Consumer complaint websites can create public embarrassment for the company, such as **www.ripoffreport. com** and **www.consumeraffairs.com**.

Save on Medical Needs

Try generic and over-the-counter drugs

Medicine is not necessarily a "you get what you pay for" situation. Many generic versions may work as well as their more expensive counterparts.

Check with your health insurance provider

Before you get your annual physical checkup, bi-annual dental cleaning, etc., call your health insurance provider to confirm that the visit will be covered by your policy. If you receive a serious health diagnosis, ask your health insurance provider to assign a "case manager" to you. That manager can help you qualify for additional services.

Carry your health insurance card at all times

You need your health insurance card to receive care efficiently in an emergency. The card also helps assure that you will be billed properly. In an emergency, try to obtain pre-approval from your carrier for your treatment, if at all possible.

Be forewarned that some health insurance providers won't insure services provided at certain hospitals or doctors' offices. This would be the case if the hospital or doctor doesn't have a contract to get paid by the provider. For example, at one time, the health insurance coverage for Heidi's two sons was no longer accepted by the hospital near their home.

Payment for any treatment you receive is ultimately your responsibility. If the treatment you receive isn't covered by your insurance, you will have to pay for the treatment yourself. Try to get pre-approval whenever you can.

Be an active participant in your health care

Every time you visit a doctor, bring a list of questions. Write down the answers. When a doctor orders a test or procedure, ask if it is really necessary and if so, why? If it's a redo of a test, why does the test need to be repeated? Could repeats be dangerous to your health? You deserve the answers to these questions. It's your body and your wallet—not the doctor's!

Stay on top of the details

We hope that you never have to enter a hospital as a patient. If you do, try to obtain a notepad and make as many notes as you can. If you are in no condition to do so, ask a friend or family member to ask questions and take notes for you. This journal will help empower you in your care and serve as a valuable record.

When you check in, you may be required to give the staff your personal items, such as your wallet and jewelry. List all your personal items and their value on your notepad. Ask for a receipt and hang on to it. This will help ensure that you will receive all your possessions when you are allowed to have them.

Write down the names of the tests you receive and who recommended them. Keep a list of the location and duration of any pain and symptoms you may feel. When doctors and nurses check on your condition, write down their names and what they told you.

Get a patient's representative at the hospital

A patient's representative is an advocate provided for you at some hospitals. Ask to be introduced to him or her as soon as possible. Get all of their available contact information. He or she should be able to pass along your complaints or suggestions to the proper authorities. This can save you money by eliminating miscommunication and perhaps shortening your stay at the hospital.

Review your bill

Before you check out of the hospital, you may receive a hospital bill. Study it carefully. Be sure to get a fully itemized version of the bill, even though it may be pages long. Call the billing office of the hospital to request an explanation of charges that don't make sense or that could be errors. Dispute any charges that don't coordinate with your records. If you have a dispute, call your insurance provider. If your employer has an insurance department, they may be able to help your dispute, also. Don't sign off on a bill until you are satisfied it is correct.

Be sure to save all receipts, billing, and documentation for your medical expenses for your tax preparer or accountant. This will help you get all allowed deductions for medical expenses.

Get the best

Not all doctors are created equal. Get the best medical care that you can afford. It could be a matter of life and death. If you feel that one doctor isn't listening to you or doesn't really understand your situation, ask for a second opinion from another doctor. If you're not satisfied with the second doctor, see a third doctor. Always check with your carrier first. Even HMO insurance plans allow for a second opinion.

Recently a friend of Heidi's got three opinions. The first three doctors each gave her a different medicine, each for a different illness. But she still didn't know what was making her sick. Finally, she found a fourth doctor. He took a different test that uncovered the problem. Fortunately, Heidi's friend followed her "gut" instinct and kept searching for the cause of her illness. Otherwise, she would have been taking medicines for an incorrect diagnosis, which would have made her condition even worse.

Save the best way on medical needs

The best way to save on medical needs is to not need them in the first place! Get in good health and stay in good health with lots of exercise, sleep, and wholesome food. Avoid stress and eliminate any addictions. Bring as much love and laughter into your life as possible.

To take the time to exercise is a challenge. But it's so very important. We try to practice what we preach. Sam has a personal trainer who comes to his house several times a week. Other days, he walks on his treadmill. Heidi and her husband lift weights at their local YMCA together in the mornings and take walks together in the evenings.

To start the exercise routine that works best for you, visit all the fitness clubs in your area and compare their prices and amenities. Depending on where you live, YMCAs, YWCAs, and other clubs can provide athletic facilities at reasonable rates.

Wherever and however you get your exercise, get out there, get going, and don't stop!

It's not your wealth;
it's your health.

Chapter 16

SAVING TIPS
FOR TRAVEL AND ENTERTAINMENT

"It is not so hard to earn money as to spend it well."
—Spurgeon

Travel and entertainment make life worthwhile. You can't eliminate them from your life. Instead, find new, less expensive ways to enjoy trips with your loved ones and enjoyable times with your friends.

Save on Travel

Know why you are taking the vacation

The quality of a vacation is not based on how much money you spend. What counts most is the enjoyment, deepened relationships, and happy memories that the trip creates. Approach your vacation from the philosophy of *TheSmartestWay*™. Ask yourself, "How will this trip enrich my life and my relationships? What is the best way for me and them to spend quality time?"

When you plan a trip with your loved ones, schedule plenty of "bonding time." If you have younger children, this is what they will remember most. They won't remember how much money you spent at an expensive restaurant, but they will remember that on the way to the restaurant, you stopped the car by the beach and suggested that you all sit on the sand together to watch the sunset.

One of the best vacations in Heidi's childhood started with a disaster. The family station wagon broke down on the way to their destination. The repairs took several days, but the auto insurance company paid for the nicest motel in town. To her delight, the motel had a swimming pool. The relaxed afternoons playing in the pool with her family became a fond memory.

Know where to go

Your destination is a factor how much you will spend on your vacation. Have you explored all the enjoyable activities that your city or your state has to offer? If you don't want to spend extra money on gas or airline tickets, you can still have a memorable vacation. Here's how: reserve a nice room at the best hotel in your town or the nearest city. Pretend you are a tourist. Lay by the pool, stroll through an art museum, eat at a top restaurant, enjoy a drink at a jazz bar, and attend a concert. Rediscover your city by taking an historical walking tour or bus tour.

Your local automobile club, chamber of commerce, and community tourism offices can suggest nearby excursions. Check with your state tourism office to find all the activities and destinations in your state. Most of these offices have websites, too.

You can even invite friends or relatives to join you for your low-cost "getaway." You can reduce hotel costs by sharing rooms with two queen beds or one-bedroom suites at hotels such as **www.embassysuites.com**, **www.residenceinn.com**, **www. homesteadhotels.com**, **www.amerisuites.com**, and **www. radisson.com**. You all may have even more fun than you would have if you had spent twice the time and money traveling to another state or country.

If hotel rates are beyond your budget, day-trips are available in your area. Explore your nearby national and state parks. Borrow some camping gear and sleep under the stars. Children enjoy outdoor activities such as hiking, building a campfire, and roasting marshmallows with their family. It's the memories, not the miles.

Know how to get a bargain

When you travel, you will spend extra money, so plan ahead and stretch your travel budget. Comparison shop on the Internet. Use discount travel sites such as Trip Advisor **www.tripadvisor.com, www.orbitz.com, www.expedia. com, www.travelocity.com, www.hotels.com,** and **www. priceline.com** for bargains on rental cars.

With rental cars, you may not need to buy insurance. Call your auto insurance provider to find out if your insurance protects you in the case of an accident while driving a rental car. Find out if your coverage is for a limited number of days traveling or if is limited to just the United States.

Membership with automobile and recreational vehicle associations may entitle you to a free magazine about traveling. For example, members of AAA of California **www.aaa-calif. com** receive Westways Magazine, which contains suggestions for California drivers on how to save while traveling.

Know how to negotiate with hotels

When you book a room at a hotel, you may be asked for a credit card to hold the reservation. Confirm that your credit card will not be billed before you check in. Also confirm the cancellation policy and make a note of it.

When you book your room, always ask, "Can I get a better rate?" Recently, Heidi made a hotel reservation. She asked if she could get a discount or upgrade because she is an AAA member. Hotels often shave a few dollars off the price of the room if you are an AAA member. To her delight, the hotel offered her a junior suite on the executive level, free valet parking, and breakfast.

Also ask, "Can I get an upgrade at no charge?" Often, the hotel reservation operator will say that he or she cannot commit to an upgrade but will put in a request. Remember, when you check into the hotel, to ask for a no-charge upgrade. Ask, "Can my room be upgraded at no extra charge?" Ask if the hotel has an executive level or concierge level. Some hotels have executive-level or concierge-level lounges that provide computers, printers, big screen televisions, coffee, other beverages, appetizers, and desserts.

Lastly, ask for early check-in and late check-out when you make the reservation. These usually are not guaranteed, but they are no-cost upgrades that extend your vacation time. The fact is, many guest rooms are ready to be occupied by 10:00 a.m. Some hotels are willing to extend the required checkout time to 4:00 p.m. This extra time would allow you to schedule a nap after a morning sightseeing and lunch. As we like to remind you, it never hurts to ask. If you don't ask for the upgrades, someone else will get them.

Know where your wallet is

Watch for pickpockets and credit card thieves. When you're traveling, you're distracted by finding your way around, seeing the sights, keeping track of your luggage, and talking with your traveling companions. When you are in an unfamiliar environment, it's easy to lose track of your wallet or credit cards. Thieves know this.

Some people wear a "dummy wallet" with $20 in it. They keep their real wallet in a special travel pouch or their sock. If you wear a fanny-pack, find one that has a hidden clip-hook and steel-enforced webbing so that the fanny pack can't be easily unclipped or cut off your waist by a thief.

Whenever you use your credit card, remember to check four things: 1) are you being charged for the right amount? 2) did you get your receipt? 3) did you get your credit card back?, and 4) is the card actually yours?

Traveler's checks may seem like a good idea. However, many people don't bother to redeem leftover checks after the trip is finished. This is not productive use of their money.

Know how to plan for "holds"

Many major hotels put a mandatory "hold" on your credit card when you check in. The hold is a predetermined amount of funds per day, perhaps $75. The hold amount varies with each hotel. This amount is the "estimated average incidental charges" you might incur and charge to your room each day during your stay. Examples of these charges are snacks and beverages from your room's mini-bar, dining in the hotel's restaurants, and dry cleaning services at the hotel.

When you check into a hotel, find out what the hold amount is and when it will be billed to your account. Each hotel has a different policy. The hold shouldn't affect your ability to charge on the card unless you've reached your credit limit. Plan ahead so that your credit card doesn't max out.

Don't use a debit card to check into a hotel. At least one worldwide hotel chain withdraws the hold amount for your entire stay from your checking account as soon as you check in with your debit card. For example, if you are checking into a hotel that requires a daily hold of $75, and you are checking in for a four-day visit, a grand total of $300 will be withdrawn from your checking account immediately.

If you don't spend $75 per day in incidentals at the hotel each day, you will get a refund of the remaining balance. Here's the kicker: at least one hotel chain doesn't return the refund to your checking account until 72 hours after you check out of the hotel. Some hotel guests have found that the incidentals charges were not paid back until over a week after they checked out of the hotel.

If you absolutely must use a debit card at a hotel, make sure it contains sufficient funds so the daily charges don't empty your account or cause penalties. After your trip, remember to call your bank or credit union to make sure that refund was returned to your account.

The best way to find out about a hotel's policy is to ask. If the hotel clerk cannot explain it to you, talk to the manager. Ask questions until you get a clear understanding of the policy. Then make notes that can be followed up on later. Yes, the money in your account belongs to you. But when you hand over your debit card, the hotel can take any amount of your money whenever it chooses to and return your money when it's convenient.

Know how to check out of the hotel

When you check out of the hotel, examine your bill before you agree to it. The local taxes, bed taxes, and government taxes may take your breath away. Then there are the costs for parking, in-room snacks, rentals for movies and video games, room service, and phone calls. Make sure that you agree to all the charges listed. Ask the manager to remove the errors from your bill and give you a corrected bill for your records.

If there were any problems with the room, such as no warm water in the morning for showering, tell the manager about it. Be insistent and you may receive free breakfast or a free night's stay.

Know how to prevent unintended charges

Watch for unintended hotel charges, such as phone calls and snacks.

To call out from your hotel room can be very expensive. In some hotels, the charge for one quick phone call is almost $10. Use your cell phone for out-going calls. Incoming calls should be free, but check with your hotel to make sure.

Many hotels have a mini-bar, a small refrigerator filled with drinks and snacks in the room. When you check into your room, the hotel clerk may offer you a mini-bar key. If you refuse to take the key, you won't be tempted to snack on the hotel's wildly overpriced snacks. It's better to bring your own snacks.

If you are disciplined, you can get the key, empty the hotel drinks out of the refrigerator, and use it to keep your own food and beverages cool. You could even buy milk, juice, and cereal at a local market and eat breakfast in your room.

The snacks in your room are not free. Some hotels display the snacks and drinks on a special electronic tray plugged into an electrical outlet. If you remove those tasty treats from the tray for a few moments, a sensor automatically bills your room.

Always remember to analyze your hotel bill for unintended charges when you check out.

Save on Entertainment

Look for new ways to enjoy yourself

"A fool and his money are soon parted," can be put another way: "A fool and his money are soon partying." It's time to trim your entertainment budget. Here are ways to be money-wise and still have fun.

Do you miss evenings of dining out? Make something special to eat at home. It may taste even better than a restaurant dish and will surely cost less. Don't want to spend money on cookbooks? The Internet is full of recipes for every skill level and every ingredient.

When you do go to a restaurant as a treat, there are ways to save. One way is to split your meal with one of your dining partners. Another way is to stretch your meal. Most restaurants will give provide an extra plate so you can share your salad, entrée, and dessert. If you have food left over, ask for a "doggy bag" so you can take it home. Restaurant leftovers are usually tasty the next day. No money for a full dinner? Go to the restaurant later in the evening and tell the hostess quietly that you are there "just for dessert tonight." She will gladly seat you.

The whole family can eat economically at family style buffet restaurants. For locations near you, visit **www.buffets.com**, **www.souplantation.com** and search on the Internet under "all-you-can-eat restaurants."

Do you miss going to the movies? You can check out DVDs and VHS videos for free at the library. You can buy them for a dollar or two at thrift stores. If you are sick at home or have lots of time to watch movies, give Netflix **www.netflix.com** a try. You can have a two-week trial membership for free and choose from thousands of movies.

If you do go to the movie theater, don't pay for high-priced snacks. Seriously, how can a bucket of popcorn really be worth $7? Heidi and her husband stock up on their favorite "movie candy" whenever they visit the 99 Cent Store **www.99only. com**. If your theater allows it, simply carry in a can of soda and a box of candy in your purse or pocket. What you save in snacks can be used toward another evening at the movies, so everyone wins.

Look for something interesting to do

Find an inexpensive hobby or sports you enjoy. Attend classes and lectures at your local community college and your library to broaden your interests and skills and make new friends.

Are you in the mood for some intellectual or cultural stimulation? When was the last time you visited your local museums? Contact your local library and community affairs office for free classes and presentations on history and travel. Bring a picnic to the park to enjoy free concerts and art fairs.

Throw creative parties

People love to attend parties. Your parties can have a theme, such as toga, luau, western, disco, fifties, etc. Co-ed pajama parties are lots of laughs, because everyone wears their pajamas and plays Charades, Monopoly, Twister, or other old-fashioned kid games. Spa parties are an inexpensive alternative to "girls' night out." A home skin-care line demonstrator gives each guest a facial, while the other guests give each other manicures and pedicures.

Instead of a theme, your party can have a purpose, such as for friends leaving on vacation (a bon voyage party), returning from a trip (a welcome back party), renewing wedding vows (a re-confirmation party), or celebrating a return to health (a recovery party). Heidi has a friend who throws a party every year to celebrate her anniversary of yet another year of being free from breast cancer.

Ask for what you want

Restaurants can be helpful when planning a party. It never hurts to ask. One of Heidi's favorite Los Angeles restaurants allows her to hold parties in their private dining room at reasonable prices. The large, elegant room serves 8–20 sitting down. To reserve the room for two hours, she only has to commit to spend $160 in food and beverages, for example a total of eight guests each spending $20.

Restaurants love to cater your home parties and picnics, too. That way, no one has to spend time in the kitchen. Let your favorite restaurant know what you want, and they will be glad to work out the details economically for you.

Don't be too proud to potluck

Heidi's favorite method of home entertaining is potluck. This saves time, money, and hassle for the hostess. Each guest brings something—a salad, an entrée, a vegetable dish, some meat to grill, bread, beverages, or dessert—so there is usually enough food for everyone, even if you don't know how many guests will attend. Just to be safe, you can provide the main course of barbeque, or a big pot of stew, chili, or spaghetti. You can suggest a popular food theme, such as Mexican or Italian food.

Most guests are glad to pitch in. If they are short on time, they can pick up dessert and wine from a deli or grocery store. Many people enjoy sharing their favorite dishes. The food becomes a topic of conversation.

If you have a big family or lots of friends who gather frequently, how about starting a tradition of a regular potluck brunch or dinner? You could set the date as the second Sunday of every month, alternating at each other's homes. To spice up the conversation, you could ask everyone to bring a "share time" item, like in elementary school. The share item could be reading a poem, playing a piece of music, or telling the story about a family photograph.

Save on invitations

The cost of professionally printed invitations goes up all the time. Sometimes event planners spend as much on the invitations as they do on the entire event. This is a waste of money because few people save their invitations. Why not spend the money instead on something more memorable, such as entertainment or table gifts?

Invitations can be creative, memorable, and inexpensive. If most of your guests use email, invite them online with Evite **www.evite.com**. Evite has hundreds of creative, classy, pre-designed email invitations for every possible occasion. You can send an unlimited number of invitations entirely free.

For paper invitations, search craft stores such as Michaels **www.michaels.com**, scrap-booking stores, and the Internet for ideas for creative, handmade invitations. Home color printers can print attractive, customized invitations. Maybe a friend can help you design them. Wedding invitation kits include matching satin-trimmed cards, sheer velum sheets, envelopes, and small, matching RSVP cards and envelopes to be inserted into the invitation. These can be printed on a home black ink printer.

To save on postage, the U.S. Postal Service sometimes offers discounts for mail sent nearby. You can also get volume discounts or purchase Express Mail online at a discount at **www.usps. com**.

Save on food

Your food at your party can be delicious and bountiful without busting your budget. Visit your local Smart and Final store **www.smartandfinal.com**, Costco **www.costco.com**, or Sam's Club **www.samsclub.com** for party-size portions and wine. World Market **www.worldmarket.com** carries unusual imported gourmet items. If you are fortunate enough to have a Trader Joe's store **www.traderjoes.com** nearby, you will find gourmet food, great wine, and alcohol at bargain prices.

Save on party decorations

Visit party supply stores in your area, such as Party City **www. partycity.com** and Party America **www.partyamericastore. com**. Search the Internet, including Evite **www.evite.com** for inexpensive ideas for party themes, food, decorations, and table gift ideas. If your birthday is near a holiday, use that holiday as your theme. For example, Heidi's birthday is just before Valentine's Day, one of her favorite holidays.

Stores such as Michaels **www.michaels.com** and Joann Fabric and Craft Stores **www.joann.com** also have crafts for making invitations, place cards, decorations, and centerpieces. IKEA **www.ikea.com** has inexpensive, clever table gifts, centerpiece ideas, and creative lighting suggestions.

Decorate chairs with wide bows made with strips of fabric that match or coordinate with the tablecloths, table runners, and napkins that you make. Bed sheets make wonderful tablecloths and napkins. You don't need a sewing machine, just a good pair of pinking shears scissors. Keep an eye on flyers for sales at stores such as Joann Fabric and Craft Stores **www.joann.com** and decorator fabric stores such as Calico Corners **www. calicocorners.com**. Sign up for coupons to be emailed to you from these stores. Also, the Internet lists dozens of fabric sources.

Here's an idea for the easiest and showiest floral display for your centerpiece or coffee table: Go to your local farmers' market and buy an armload of lilies. Asian lilies last a long time. Buy buds that are still closed. Clip the bottoms of the stems, keep the water fresh, and the buds will open in time for your party, fill the room with fragrance, and last for a week or two.

Save on decorating for your party

If your party inspires you to give your home a facelift, you can do it easily if you have a sewing machine and can sew a straight line. Create pillow covers, drapes, duvet covers, and throw-blankets. You can cover an ugly wall or odd view with a drapery that covers the entire wall. Remember that bed sheets on sale provide large amounts of inexpensive, attractive, durable fabric.

Paint gives an inexpensive but creative new look. Your local community college will have helpful decorating classes, such as painting decorative faux finishes. Buy attractive but inexpensive area rugs at Lowe's **www.lowes.com** or Home Depot **www.homedepot.com**. Buy dried flower arrangements at craft stores such as Michaels **www.michaels.com**, Joann Fabric and Craft Stores **www.joann.com** and Wal-Mart **www.walmart.com**. Shop for unusual accessories at annual sales at furniture stores for unusual accessories. Watch television channels about home decorating such as HGTV (Home and Garden TV) **www.hgtv.com**, and DIY (Do It Yourself Network) **www.diynetwork.com**.

Stick to your party budget

Determine your budget for your party and stick to it. You can always substitute less expensive items or eliminate items to keep your bottom line.

Sam's parties are larger and more formal than Heidi's parties. If he uses a caterer, banquet manager, or party planner, he makes sure that they work within his budget. Keep in mind that they usually receive a commission on products and services you buy. That means that the more money they convince you to spend, the more money they make for themselves. Therefore, they have very little motivation to keep your costs down.

Before you sign any contracts for your party, make sure you are agreeing to every detail about the event. The contracts should clearly state what you are buying and the total amount to you will pay and when. If any problems arise later, those contracts will decide the issue, in your favor you hope. Keep your copy handy.

Substitute when you can

Be sure to consider all possible food and flower options. You can have high appeal with low cost if you are creative. Remember that when certain fruits, vegetables, and flowers are out of season, they cost more. Find out what are in season and use them instead. This is a good idea, even if you aren't planning a party.

You can also save on desserts. Many banquet halls suggest an elaborate dessert. Sam has observed, however, that about half to three-quarters of the guests don't eat their desert or they only take a bite or two. If it's a birthday or anniversary, have a big cake that is then cut into modest-size pieces. Let the hotel or banquet hall know that you do not want the pieces cut too large. Then welcome guests to come to the cake table and take a piece of cake if they want it. If there is cake left over, the catering staff can walk around the room with trays of cake pieces.

Many guests will refuse to take the cake because they are too busy talking, too full from dinner, or on a diet. There's no need for you to pay for beautiful, overpriced desserts that will be tossed in the trash barrel. For weddings, of course, don't offer a dessert in addition to the wedding cake. That would be "sweet-tooth overkill."

Know for how many to book the room

When you make reservations for a large party or wedding, you may be concerned about how many guests will actually show up. Event planners estimate that roughly 10% to 15% of the people who say they will attend do not actually show up. Here is a tip that can save you lots of money on your event budget. Banquet halls often allow you an additional 10% leeway on the number of guests they serve. Check with your banquet coordinator.

Let's say you are expecting 198 guests. Don't make the reservation for 198 guests. Here's why: if you book the hall for 180 guests, the hall will be prepared to serve 198, an additional 10%. If more than 180 arrive, you pay for each additional meal individually, per person. This costs less than agreeing to pay for

198 guests and have fewer than 198 of the guests show up, because you would have to pay for 198 dinners, even if fewer guests arrive.

Know how to get a bargain

Not all of Sam's social events have been lavish affairs. When he was a student at Stanford University, he ran an off-campus boarding house one year. To raise extra money for the boarding house, he offered a Saturday night "all you can eat" dinner for about 125 people. The boarding house served spaghetti with meat sauce, garlic bread, salad, and a mug full of beer (but the students had to bring their own mug). Sam bought hamburger in bulk for 10¢ a pound and cheddar cheese for 10¢ a pound. The charge for dinner was $1.25, but the cost of the food was less than 50¢ per meal.

For a change of pace, once he bought lamb riblets on sale for 10¢ a pound. To make them edible, he marinated then over-night in teriyaki soy sauce and broiled them. The boarding house got four orders to a pound and sold them for 25¢ per order. They sold an average of $1.00 worth of riblets to each of the Saturday night guests. Those little riblets added up to big profits by the end of the evening.

That was in 1954. Even today, however, buying in bulk and being creative with your menu can result in an elaborate affair at a reasonable price.

Ask the pros for advice

When you start planning your party, know the number of guests and the type of food. Then ask grocery store managers for advice about what to serve and how to prepare it.

You never know who will come to your rescue. While at Stanford, Sam belonged to a club on campus. One year, the club was required to host about 900 people for an alumni reception after one of the football games. The club had only $100 in its bank account. The club members asked the campus commissary cooks for help. The cooks told them about a beverage flavoring powder they could buy in bulk for about $20. It made enough punch to serve 900 people. They purchased napkins and paper cups at a discount store and spent about $5 on fresh fruit. In those days $5 could buy quite a few apples, oranges, and peaches. They cut the fruit into small pieces and sprinkled it on the top of the punch.

The event cost less than $100. The Alumni Association said it was one of the most successfully catered receptions that any campus organization had put on for them, even though some of the other receptions had much larger budgets.

**It's not how much you spend for fun;
it's how much fun you have.**

Chapter 17

HOW TO BE A THRIFTY SHOPPER

*"A cynic is a man who knows the price of everything
and the value of nothing."*
—Oscar Wilde

Most people have lots of experience in shopping, but not everyone knows the best ways to shop. Here's how to increase the value of your purchases while decreasing the amount that you spend on them.

Search for value

Know value when you find it. Look for real value, not flashy packaging. Invest your money in long-term quality, not temporary prestige. Don't be fooled into thinking that designer brand items are higher in quality. An item isn't necessarily higher quality just because it has a famous label. This holds true for almost everything, including jewelry, furniture, tableware, linens, and cars.

Some things have real value and are worth the price. On that list are healthful food, comfortable shoes, well-made beds, and sturdy furniture.

Analyze your purchase

Whenever you find something you want, analyze it closely before you buy. Don't forget to adopt *TheSmartestWay*™ philosophy and ask yourself: "Do I really need this?" "Is it priced well?" "Is it made well?" "Can I afford it?" "Will I use it often?" "Does it work with other things I own?" "Will I be able to use it several years from now?" "Does it really have value for me?"

If you answer "no" to any of these questions, don't buy it.

Sam's stories about value

Sam learned to look for real value when he was young. Once he visited his cousin who was working as a butcher in a supermarket. In the display case was ground sirloin for $1.50 per pound and hamburger for $1.00 per pound. Sam asked his cousin, "What is the difference between the ground sirloin and the hamburger?" His cousin replied, honestly, "50¢ a pound."

Sam's father was a manufacturer of vitamins for most of the major drug chains on the West Coast. One of his customers was a high-end pharmacy that sold his multi-vitamin formula in a green capsule for $16 a bottle. Another customer was a large chain of discount drug stores. They sold the same multi-vitamins in a red capsule for $8 a bottle. Each bottle contained the same number of capsules. Sam once asked his father, "What is the difference between what the pharmacy is selling and what the discount drug store is selling?" His father replied simply, "One capsule is green and the other is red." From this, Sam learned that the most expensive is not always better.

Think before you spend

Shop with a list. Shop intentionally, not aimlessly. Before you buy, ask the *TheSmartestWay*™ questions, "What am I trying to accomplish with this purchase?" "Is this purchase going to help me save money in the long run?" "Is this the best use of my money right now?" "Does this purchase help me reach my long-range goals?"

Ask for the bargain price

If you don't ask, you don't get. Sam's wife always asks the "magic" question, "What can you do for us on this?" Then she asks a second time, just as politely, "Isn't there something more you can do?"

It may feel a bit awkward at first, but you'll start to get a thrill from the "magic" results of simply asking. With each new perk or discount that you receive, you will become more confident and remember to ask more often.

According to a recent study, over 90% of people who asked for a discount received at least one discount. This technique even applies to legal and medical bills. Don't be too proud to let your doctors and lawyers know that you need them to please "shave a little off the top" of their bill. Many hospitals will work with you on payment plans, also.

Many expensive items have a large markup in price. Therefore, the store can afford to give you a 5% to a 15% discount. On luxury items such as jewelry, the discount may be 50%–60%. But a store won't give you a discount unless you ask for it.

If you have a taste for fine jewelry, analyze whether it is really the best use of your money or if you can make a more profitable investment elsewhere. It's difficult to know if the value of jewelry will increase over time.

Know who to ask and how to ask

You are more likely to get a lower price when you ask the owner or manager rather than a sales associate. Always ask, "Can you do better?" Stay upbeat but persistent. If you escalate your request beyond what is realistic, the manager may politely withdraw from the negotiation and you will have lost the chance to save money.

When you ask for a discount, remember that the sales associate or manager has to answer to his or her boss. Perhaps the boss wants to reduce excess merchandise before an inventory. This situation would encourage motivation to bargain. Perhaps he or she is not allowed to give you a discount on the model you want, but can discount an older model.

You often don't need the very newest model of electronics and other items. Usually the slightly older model is good enough and perhaps even more reliable. It has been out on the market longer and tested by more users.

In some cases, the store may not be able to offer you a discount on the item itself but may have floor samples or discontinued models. The floor models may have a slight defect that doesn't affect the purpose, appearance, or usefulness of the item. The same is sometimes true with clothing in a department store. For appliances, ask a contractor what is the most reliable and properly priced brand for your needs. Choose a reliable brand for the price.

Try to buy expensive items at discount stores. The savings can be substantial, but you need to make sure that it is a true discount. Compare the discount price with the lowest price you can get from a regular store. Sears **www.sears.com**, JC Penney **www.jcpenney.com**, Target **www.target.com**, Kohl's **www. kohls.com**, and other discount stores are good places to start comparison shopping.

Use senior discounts

Speaking of discounts, remember that when you reach age fifty-five, you qualify for a senior discount at some movie theatres and restaurants. An increasing number of stores and movie theatres provide discounts for people over age fifty-five, students, or veterans. Are you part of a group that receives discounts? If so, don't hesitate to ask for what you deserve. Heidi points out that you could save enough to buy popcorn. Sam says, skip the popcorn and add the money to your savings account!

Keep price tags and receipts

Keep the receipts for your purchases. Keep the original boxes, bags, and wrapping. Don't cut the price tags off items until you are really sure that you want to keep the item. You could change your mind for several reasons. Perhaps the item doesn't fit your budget, doesn't coordinate with your other things, or a sales person or so-called friend convinced you to buy it. After you buy a pair of shoes, test them at home for awhile. Wear the shoes only on a rug so you don't scuff the soles--and you can return them if necessary.

You may want to return an item if you find it at a lower price somewhere else. In shopping as in life, keep your options open as much as possible. If you are making a sizeable purchase, get the name of the sales associate. That way, you can ask him or her to help you if there is a problem or you need to make a return.

Sometimes, gift givers are courteous enough to give you a "gift receipt" when they give you a gift. You should do the same. This allows the receiver to return the item to the store and buy something else. No one should feel guilty about exchanging gifts. It's better for everyone to be happy about the gift rather than to keep something just in order to not hurt anyone's feelings.

Ask for what you deserve

You must learn to be a proactive, assertive customer. Don't be afraid to return merchandise you don't want for fear that a sales associate may dislike you or act rudely to you. Remember, in retail, "The customer is king (or queen)."

Be bold when you ask for a refund for faulty merchandise. It's not your fault if the merchandise is unsatisfactory, so don't apologize for it. Also, you have the right to demand that unapproved charges be removed from your credit card bill. Someone else made the error and they need to correct it.

You won't get what you deserve unless you ask. So ask.

Use clubs, catalogs, discount cards

Many grocery stores, drug stores, bookstores, and other retailers offer customers a "frequent customer" discount card. Some have an annual charge for the membership, but most are free. For stores that charge for membership, decide if you will save more than the amount of annual charge, if you shop at the store. If you forget or misplace your discount card, many stores will have your information in their database or they will swipe a generic discount card for you, so that you get discounts.

Beware of warranties and early entrants

Extended warranties are frequently offered on appliances and technology devices. Stores love to offer them because they represent $9 billion in sales every year. However, on average, for every 100 warranties sold, only 15 people make claims. Take your time before deciding on an extended warranty.

If the item is low cost and you could buy a new one for close to the price of the warranty, don't buy the warranty. Sometimes the warranty may cost more than the repairs would be if you were to need them. Many major appliances are well made and seldom need repairs during the life of the extended warranty.

Check to make sure that your item already has a manufacturer's coverage for the first thirty days or the first year. You usually have thirty days to decide to purchase a warranty if you change your mind and decide to buy one. Ask the sales associate about this.

An "early entrant" is the first offer of the fresh-from-the-factory model. Often the first introduction of an item is priced higher than later versions. Waiting a little time can save you a lot of money, especially on electronics.

Shop early—or late

Often you can save on airline tickets and hotel reservations by buying early. You can choose from a better selection if you go to garage sales and flea markets early in the morning.

You may find something you like that seems overpriced. If so, try to come back at the end of the day and offer a lower price, if it is still there. Quite often the seller will deeply discount anything that is left at the end of the day.

When visiting a trade show or arts festival, the same is often true of merchandise that is left at the end of the show. The vendor may not want to take it home and will either give it away or sell it at a deep discount.

In other situations, buying as late as possible can save quite a bit of money. A good example is a new car or major appliance. You can usually get a good discount if you buy a car or appliance at the end of the model year. That's when the new models are about to come out and the dealer is eager to clear out the older models.

Shop at the end of the holiday season for real savings. The best time to buy any holiday items is the day after that holiday. The selection is still good and the prices are even better—usually half off or more. Stock up for next year's decorations and handy gifts.

The best time to buy office supplies is in August during back-to-school sales. Almost everything is on sale at office supply stores at that time.

Shop for sales

It also pays to wait for sales. Sam buys his shirts and suits from a very high-end department store that has sales twice a year. By waiting for the sales, he usually saves 25%–30%. When he sees an item that he needs, he asks when it will be on sale and when the next sale is scheduled. Note the sales dates on your calendar and start compiling a list of the items that you need to shop for at those sales.

January is a great month for sales because stores try to get rid of last year's and holiday merchandise. Year round, some stores such as Borders Books **www.borders.com** and Barnes and Noble **www.barnesandnoble.com** have specific areas for bargain-priced items. Look for designated areas for discounted merchandise at furniture stores, such as IKEA **www.ikea.com**.

Look for stores that are going out of business or liquidating inventory. But before you go crazy with sales, become a shopper *TheSmartestWay*™ and first decide: "Am I really saving money on things I need? Or am I using the sale as an excuse to buy things I don't need?"

Comparison shop

Do your research before you lay down your hard-earned money for big-ticket items such as electronics and cars. Ask people whom you respect for their recommendations. If they have already purchased the item, ask them *TheSmartestWay*™ questions: How do they like it? Do they wish that they had bought a different model? Where did they find the best bargain? Also check Consumer Reports magazine and online at **www.consumerreports.org** to find information and ratings about all kinds of products.

Comparison shop for bargains on the Internet, too. In your search engine, type the product you are looking for and the word "discount." Numerous websites will appear. Also, some sites help you find all the discount sites for each kind of product you may be seeking. Remember, good quality can be obtained at a good price.

When you enter a store, briefly walk around the store and observe everything. Then compare products and prices with other stores before you make a decision to purchase. Make sure you are getting the best value and you are getting what you really want within your budget.

Almost every weekend, Sam likes to comparison shop at local farmers' markets, swap meets, and flea markets. These are places where lots of vendors are selling similar merchandise. He has found that the vendors located nearer the entrance often charge a higher price than those farther away from the entrance. So Sam tours the entire market and makes mental notes about products and prices before he buys anything. He always saves money by comparison shopping first.

It's not what you buy;
it's how you shop.

Chapter 18

WHERE TO SHOP TO FIND GOOD DEALS

"Almost any man knows how to earn money,
but not one in a million knows how to spend it."
—Henry David Thoreau

Our country is filled with malls and stores. The options to spend money can seem limitless. Where you shop determines if you will find what you need—and save money at the same time.

Shop at dollar stores and farmers' markets

As mentioned earlier, visit your local dollar stores like 99 Cent Only stores **www.99only.com**, Dollar Stores **www.dollarstore.com**, and Dollar Tree Stores **www.dollartree.com**. These stores offer many everyday products, as well as gifts and holiday items. As always, be sure to examine your purchases carefully to make sure they are the quality you need.

At farmers' markets, sometimes the prices are higher than at a grocery store. But often the produce is fresher, tastier, and may be organic.

Shop at garage sales and thrift shops

Garage sales and swap meets are intriguing places to pick up odds-and-ends. "One person's trash is another person's treasure." Consignment shops that sell furniture or clothes provide great shopping.

You can sell your unwanted items through an advertisement in the classifieds section of your newspaper and the free local Penny Saver catalogs. "Turn your trash into cash" and resell the extra stuff in your life that is weighing you down and holding you back. "Monetize" those items so you can buy what you really need. The Internet offers trading and swapping opportunities, such as Craig's List **www.craigslist.org**.

Items that are difficult to sell can save you money if you donate them to a qualified, non-profit organization and take a tax deduction off their income taxes for the value of the donation. Consult with your tax preparer or accountant for details. Thrift stores and pawn shops can be worthwhile, depending on the location. Generally, the nicer neighborhoods have better merchandise. For example, thrift stores and pawn shops in or near very upscale areas, such as Beverly Hills, offer some remarkable bargains.

Don't forget your local library. You can check out movies, DVDs, CDs, audio tapes, and books for free. Some libraries may sell these items at low prices. Many are like new, and some are often in their original wrapping. Also look at **www.freecycle. com** for free stuff that people want to give away.

Shop at discount districts

Often a slightly longer drive to a wholesale clothing district, fabric district, flower district, or jewelry district is worth the extra time and money spent on gas. The "mark up"—the increase in price from wholesale to retail—is significant.

In the clothing district you may find fashion-forward, trendy items at low prices. Fabrics and flowers are found in volume discounts in their districts. The price of jewelry is often dramatically lower in the jewelry district.

Shop to upgrade your home

If you're in the market for furniture, IKEA **www.ikea.com** (800-434-IKEA) has useful, low-priced furniture, attractive home accessories, and creative kitchen and bathroom cabinetry. If you want to remodel your home, try to find a contractor or handyman who is willing to help you on his or her off-hours, evenings, and weekends, at a reduced hourly rate or project rate.

For your home office, Best Buy **www.bestbuy.com** offers bargains on technology. So does Costco, Staples **www.staples. com**, Office Max **www.officemax.com** and Office Depot **www.officedepot.com**. The discounted floor models may be just what you need at the price you want. Office supply stores also have ergonomic desks and office chairs.

Shop at auctions

Auctions are a great way to find bargains or to get rid of things you don't want anymore. Here are Sam's favorite techniques for shopping at auctions:

1. Be sure to see the item before you bid on it. Often the item will look good at first glance, but have significant defects upon closer inspection. Analyze the item up close to see if it has real value or use for you.

2. Avoid buying on impulse. Know which items you want before you attend the auction. You can usually get a catalog or review the items to be offered on the Internet. Once you start bidding, don't let your pride get in the way of your common sense. It's easy to become competitive while bidding. The goal is to get a good deal, not to beat the other bidders. The longer you bid, the harder it is to stop. Decide ahead of time the top price you are willing to pay. Bring a friend or relative and ask them to give you a tap on your shoulder when your top price is reached.

3. Develop a "poker face." A poker face is the expression a poker player wears when he wants to hide his emotions about how good or bad his cards are. In other words, don't let the other bidders know if you are glad or disappointed about how the bidding is going. Also, don't indicate what your top price is. The simplest way is to start your bid low and raise the price the minimum amount allowed.

4. Know if there is a premium. Many auctions require what is called "a buyer's premium," which ranges from 10% to 20%. For example, if the buyer's premium was 20%, for each $1.00 you bid, you would pay $1.20.

5. Add in the sales tax. Unless you have a resale license and are planning to resell the item, you must also pay sales tax on the buyer's premium. Therefore, if you bid $100 and the buyer's premium is 20% with sales tax of 6%, the item will cost you $127.20.

6. Keep income taxes in mind. Remember to calculate the full amount of income you will have to earn to pay for your auction items. As we explain elsewhere, you have to earn 160% of the price of any item you buy in order to have the necessary funds to purchase the item. Income taxes consume so much of your money and that's why you actually may have less disposable income to spend on auction items.

7. Know your shipping and repair costs. If the item is large and you need to transport it, be sure that you have the money to do so or know what it will cost to move it from the auction site to your home. If repairs are needed, have a good estimate of how much they will cost.

8. Disregard the auctioneer. Pay no attention to his or her claims about how wonderful and valuable the item is. The only thing that matters is what value it has for you and if you really need it.

9. Arrive at the auction early. The auction may run all day if there are lots of items. Find out from the auction staff approximately when the item is scheduled to come up for sale. Arrive at the auction at least half an hour prior to your item's scheduled bid time. That will give you time to examine the item closely one more time to make sure that it is still in good condition and free of defects.

10. Inquire about your storage options. If you are not going to take the item with you the day of the auction, ask how many days before you must pick it up and where it will be located. Often it will be sent to a different location after the auction.

11. Try phone bidding. At the preview, you may be able to arrange to bid by phone by filling out a form. This saves you the time and expense of another trip to the auction house.

Shop at "big box" stores

You will find some nice surprises at "big box" discount stores such as Sam's Club **www.samsclub.com**; BJs **www.bjs. com**, Big Lots **www.biglots.com**, WalMart **www.walmart. com**, and Costco **www.costco.com**. They carry quality home products, grooming basics, gift items, and casual clothes. Ask the manager for any discounts that aren't advertised. Try the "generic" store brands. Much of the merchandise in these kinds of stores is sold in larger quantities and at significant savings.

Heidi stocks up on large quantities of everyday kitchen, bathroom, and other household items, such as paper towels, facial tissue, bathroom tissue, trash bags, sandwich bags, detergent for clothes and dishes, etc. She has a pantry area in which to store them.

We want to point out that just because something is sold in quantity at a volume discount at a big box store, doesn't mean it's a true "bargain." Don't let the "bargain effect" cloud your judgment. The "bargain effect" may alter your buying decisions by convincing you to stock up on items just because they are on sale. Decide first if you really need the items and can use the larger quantities. If not, this bargain is a waste of money. On the other hand, perhaps you can split the quantities with a friend or neighbor. In any case, big box discount stores with volume quantities have much to offer.

Best Buy **www.bestbuy.com** is great place to compare prises on small appliances, televisions, cameras, computers, cell phones, and other electronics. Also, we suggest that you become acquainted with other value-oriented stores such as your local Target **www.target.com**, and Smart and Final **www. smartandfinal.com**.

*It's not where you shop;
it's what you get.*

Chapter 19

HOW TO SAVE MONEY ON CLOTHES

"What a lot of things there are a man can do without."
—Socrates

L et's face it. Most of us don't need more clothes. Most of us have enough clothes to last a long time. Still, shopping for clothes has become a popular hobby. Adults and teens flock to the malls in droves in perpetual pursuit of the "perfect" wardrobe. Advertisements tout "must-have" accessories and "to-die-for" shoes.

Figure out why clothes are so important

Have you ever asked yourself: "Why are clothes so important to me?" Some of us have motivations about our clothes that come from our childhood. Take Heidi, for example. Her mother grew up during the Depression as the youngest of nine in a thrifty, Montana farming family of Scotch descent. They knew how to make a lot from a little.

Heidi's mother encouraged her interest in fashion when she was a little girl. She would sew up unique, "couture" creations from leftover fabric whenever Heidi's Barbie dolls needed a new look. She bought Heidi dresses, petticoats, and pumps from the Salvation Army. They dyed and decorated them with ribbons and buttons for her to wear when she played "dress up."

Heidi's aunt generously mailed huge boxes full of clothes that she had lovingly sewn for her two daughters. But Heidi hated wearing "hand-me-downs" and she yearned to be "in style" and wear new clothes like the other girls at school. Her determination as a little girl grew until, as a young woman, she eventually fulfilled her dream and became an editor of a fashion publication.

Understand that you aren't what you wear

Women are especially alert to the fact that what we wear says a lot about us. But just like our car—we aren't what we drive—and we aren't what we wear either. Sometimes, it's easy to get confused about this. Here's a story related to this concept that is unfortunately all too common.

Recently a major Hollywood personality needed advice on her financial affairs. She had received a substantial income for many years, but was troubled that she had not been able to acquire any profitable investments. She confessed to her advisor that in the previous year she had spent approximately 40% of her annual after-tax income of several million dollars on clothes. She said she believed that she needed the clothes for "keeping up her image."

This story reminds Sam of the quote from another actress who was once asked, "Are you living within your income?" She replied, "No, it's all I can do to live within my credit."

Develop your own style

Create a wardrobe that is useful, unique, and makes you look and feel great. An individualized, but consistent, wardrobe style enhances your personal image. You can build on a consistent style year after year.

Experiment with and note which shapes and colors look best on you. As you develop your own style, you'll enjoy your wardrobe more. You won't need to shop as often because you will need fewer clothes. The clothes you have will work for you in more combinations and situations.

As a little girl, Heidi shopped for her clothes from the JC Penney catalog. As a young woman, she landed a job as a personal shopper for Nordstrom. There, she learned about quality and lasting style. Over time, she developed her own style that might be called California classic with a creative flair. The flair comes from her work in fashion writing.

Sam is a businessman in the conservative worlds of finance and law, so he always wears a suit and tie to the office. He was educated in the Northern California Bay Area, which is much more conservative than Southern California. In Southern California, business attire is more relaxed, so now Sam wears pale-colored shirts and pocket squares that match his tie.

Customize your look

Customize your look with individualized features.

Heidi accents her classic styled suits with trendier accessories such as scarves, unusual lapel pins, necklaces, and bracelets. She buys lapel pins from vintage clothing shops. She likes chunky stone and metal jewelry from Chico's **www.chicos.com**. She gets them on sale with coupons from the store catalog.

Find someone who knows how to sew. If Heidi buys a garment with boring buttons, she replaces them with fashionable buttons from Joann Fabric and Craft Stores **www.joann.com**. She hires a seamstress to make colorful blouses and tops from fabric that she finds at Joann stores and at discount decorator fabric stores.

Men can update and individualize their wardrobe with ties and shirts in updated patterns and fabrics. If you find a piece of fabric that would make a unique tie or shirt, take it to a seamstress. She will make a custom-fitting, one-of-a-kind piece that will cost a fraction of what you would have paid at a store.

Stick to the basics

If you buy classic styles with good quality, the core of your wardrobe won't need to be replaced as often. Buy fewer clothes but better clothes. Heidi has clothes she has worn for more than twenty years, and she still gets compliments on them. Sam buys well-made suits--on sale--so he can wear them for many years.

Men and women can keep their wardrobe budget under control by building on classic styles. First, identify the quality, classic pieces you already own. Fill in the necessary pieces of your base wardrobe, such as blazers, pants, and shirts--and skirts if you're a woman. Use only three core colors: 1. your main core color--black, gray, brown, or navy, 2. your complimentary neutral color--gray-khaki, honey-camel, or light tan, and 3. your white, either white or cream, which ever looks best on you. Classic accent colors that work well are red and royal blue, or wine and teal blue-green.

Keep a list of the items that you need to complete your core wardrobe. Shop for only those items. Shop when the season is right and the sales are on.

To update your look occasionally, add a few pieces in fashionable colors to accent your basics. These pieces can be ties and casual shirts for men, tops and accessories for women. Some trendy colors are orange, lemon, lime, pale pink, rose, magenta, lavender, purple, and turquoise.

Master the fashion trends; don't be a slave to them. Before you buy, analyze each item to decide if it coordinates with your current wardrobe, enhances your individual style, and fits your wardrobe budget.

Stay the same weight

Speaking of being consistent, one of the best ways to expand your wardrobe is to not expand your waistline. If you keep your weight the same, you can build a useful, long-term wardrobe, not two so-so wardrobes—your "fat" wardrobe and your "skinny" wardrobe.

If you can wear the same size clothes for years, it makes sense to buy quality pieces that will last.

Strategize your clothes shopping

Don't shop aimlessly. Shop with a list.

Heidi has a "plan of attack" for finding clothes at discount clothing stores. First, she wears a close-fitting T-shirt or camisole. When she enters the store, she grabs a shopping cart, courses through the store, and looks for the items on her list. If she's looking for coordinated outfits, she fills the cart with tops such as sweaters, blouses, and T-shirts that have the desired size, prices, and colors. She finds a large mirror in the store and tries on the tops over her camisole and saves the ones she likes. Then she searches the store for pants, skirts, and blazers that coordinate with those tops.

If she doesn't find bottoms to match the tops, she removes those tops from her cart. Only if she's really motivated by what's in her cart does she proceed to the dressing room.

If you have to try the clothes on in a "communal" dressing room, swallow your pride and have fun with it. Often, fellow shoppers will offer their honest opinion of how the clothes look on you.

Use the 10 Question Test

When Heidi was a personal shopper at Nordstrom, she helped women decide which clothes to buy. Since then, she has developed her own 10 Question Test. If she gets lots of "yeses" to the questions below, she puts the garment in her cart.

1. Do I really need this item?
2. Is it priced well for the value?
3. Can I afford the expense right now?
4. Would I wear it lots of places often?
5. Is it the right size?
6. Does it fit the image I'm trying to project?
7. Does it coordinate with my other clothes?
8. Is it made well enough to last several years?
9. Would I wear it several years from now?
10. Would I regret not buying it?

When she has enough garments in her cart, she heads to the dressing room. There, she decides if which clothes are flattering and comfortable and puts them in the "yes" pile. Then she asks a sales associate to put those clothes "on hold" for her until the store closes. Most stores are willing to keep items in the back room with your name on it until closing time that day. After Heidi places the items on hold, she leaves the store and runs another errand. If she's still thinking about the items an hour or two later, she might return to the store to buy them.

Know where to indulge in the thrill of the hunt

Heidi inherited the "discount-shopping gene." Her mother has always prided herself in her very attractive, thrift-store/yard-sale discoveries.

If you know where to shop, you can stretch your wardrobe budget. Everyone likes high quality and designer labels. (Actually those aren't always the same thing.). You'll be delighted with the high quality and low prices if you shop during sales and at discount stores and designer outlets. These days, you can get designer quality without the designer price. What's not to like about that?

Nordstrom, known for high quality and fashion, has an outlet store called Nordstrom Rack. Find the location nearest you online at **www.nordstrom.com** and click on the link to The Rack or call **(888-282-6060)**. The Rack sells lots of Nordstrom merchandise and has super discounts on quality underwear, shoes, clothes, and accessories for men and women. The fashions may be only a few weeks or months behind the latest fashion trends of the season.

Also, shop at outlet malls that have designer stores. Designer outlet malls are located throughout the country. Often the quality is the same as the branded merchandise found at non-outlet stores.

You'll find quality clothes at discount stores such as TJ Maxx **www.tjmaxx.com** **(800-962-MAXX)**, Loehmann's **www.loehmanns.com**, Marshall's **www.marshallsonline.com** **(800-MARSHALLS)**, Target **www.target.com** **(800-440-0680)**,

Stein Mart **www.steinmart.com**; Burlington Coat Factory **www.burlingtoncoatfactory.com**, Kohl's **www.kohls.com** (866-887-8884), JC Penney **www.jcpenney.com** (800-322-1189), Sears **www.sears.com**, and Ross Dress for Less **www.rossdressforless.com**.

As we mentioned before, you can find casual clothes at big savings at "big box" stores such as Sam's Club **www.samsclub.com**, Wal-Mart **www.walmart.com** (800-WALMART), BJ's **www.bjs.com**, and Costco **www.costco.com**.

For shoes, you can quickly try a dozen pair of shoes and find the perfect pair, if you shop at a shoe warehouse. The selection is broad and the prices low. Many of these stores, such as DSW Shoes **www.dswshoes.com**, carry discounted designer shoes and handbags. The Rack also carries shoes in large and wide sizes.

None of these stores is glamorous, but the savings can be worth the effort. Have no doubt, you can stay "in style" while discount shopping.

At this writing, these are some of the stores we recommend. Retail, however, is an industry of change. Some of these stores may be replaced by others in the future.

Care for your wardrobe

Try to buy machine-washable clothes whenever possible to save on dry cleaning bills. You might decide to try laundering certain "dry clean only" items to save money. Sometimes the garment turns out fine after being washed by hand. Hand wash delicate items in the sink with gentle soap, lay them out smooth on a towel, or hang them on a hanger. Stains come out easier with Simple Green household cleaner (full strength) or Soil Love (available at 99 Cents Only Stores).

Heidi uses a shoe repair shop to have her favorite shoes resoled. She has worn many of her shoes for years. They are comfortable, classic, and still in style. The shoe repair shop can dye her shoes and handbags to match each other or coordinate with a specific outfit.

Find a good tailor

The alterations seamstress at your dry cleaners can mend your clothes. The seamstress at Heidi's drycleaner shortens skirts and hems and alters slacks to fit better. She gives her clothes new life and keeps them fashionable.

A professional tailor or dressmaker can create custom clothes for you. Heidi designs her professional pant suits with her husband's tailor, who creates George Foreman's suits. She appreciates the quality of custom-made men's suits—the linings, the tailoring, and the covered buttons. She likes to choose from thousands of colors and patterns of fine fabrics and dozens of design styles. The suits are one-of-a-kind and fit to perfection. The best part is they cost far less than suits at fine stores!

Get beauty products at a discount

Everyone's hair, skin, and coloring are unique. Sometimes you have to pay more to get the perfect color or the correct formulation. Nevertheless, try to save when you can. Heidi tries various skin treatments from discount and drug stores, including exfoliating scrubs, self-tanning creams, and softening lotions.

A woman's hair is her crowning glory. Find the best hairstylist in town, not the most expensive hairstylist. Experiment with how long you can wait between visits. Heidi keeps her hair long and naturally wavy. Longer hair requires less trimming and highlighting. This saves both money and time. Some women color their own hair or have a friend help them.

Heidi recommends trying salon-grade shampoo and conditioner. She finds that higher-quality products help maintain manageability and color. Quality brands can be found in bulk and at a discount at beauty supply stores.

Try Heidi's low-cost "hot oil treatment" to condition your hair. Maybe it will work for your hair, too. She simply fills a plastic squeeze bottle with canola cooking oil and a few drops of mint oil extract, both from the grocery store. Once in awhile when she's in the shower, she massages a generous amount of the oil into her hair. After a few minutes, she washes the oil out with shampoo, then conditions as usual.

Try to "get what you pay for"

As we said before, a high price does not guarantee high quality. You have to be the judge of value versus price. The good news is that with careful shopping, you can get great quality at discount prices.

Nevertheless, sometimes the saying is true, "You get what you pay for." A study was done on high-quality men's dress shirts compared to lower quality. The expensive shirt lasted three times longer than the inexpensive shirt. This illustrates the concept of "cost per wear." Which shirt costs you less--the cheap one that you wear only a few times and throw away or the expensive shirt that holds up well and you wear many times?

The same is true for shoes. Better quality shoes that are comfortable can actually save you money because they last longer and prevent podiatrist bills for bunions, corns, and injuries due to tripping and slipping. This is true for men as well. Sam has some favorite shoes he has worn for over thirty years that have been re-soled four or five times.

Don't get designer-label crazy

It's not "who" you wear; it's how you look that makes an impression. A designer label is just a piece of cloth—a small piece of cloth--that you pay a lot of money for. For example, you can buy a black cashmere sweater for $100 through the Lands' End catalog **www.landsend.com** or you can pay ten times more for a similar black cashmere sweater with a designer label. It's your choice.

Sam had a client who purchased most of her clothes at one of the designer "needless mark-up" stores. Across the street was a regularly priced department store. Sam encouraged her to shop at the other store. She found several outfits for less than what she was paying for only one outfit at the higher priced store. She also purchased a wool coat at 10% of the price that she had paid for another coat at the more expensive store. Despite the fact that the less-expensive coat didn't have a designer label, she found this coat was the one she chose to wear most often.

Don't get wedding dress crazy

The perfect wedding dress seems all-important for the big day. But brides need to keep their financial sanity. Here are some ideas to help you find your dream dress and stay in your budget:

Be sentimental. A mother-of-the-bride or mother-in-law-to-be might want the bride to wear her antique wedding gown. It has a built-in heritage that honors the original wearer and her marriage. The gown could be redesigned, refitted, or updated with the help of a good tailor for far less than the cost of new gown. Plus, it will be one-of-a-kind and have loads of sentimental value.

Be persistent. In her search for the perfect wedding dress to wear when she married her husband Bill, Heidi tried on expensive gowns in many high-end bridal shops, including boutiques in Beverly Hills. She finally found her wedding ensemble at a local boutique. Her floor length, ice-blue satin skirt and corset top with matching seed pearl trim by Alfred Angelo **www.alfredangelo. com** cost only $400, full price, including her stole, satin pumps, and satin clutch, all in dyed-to-match satin.

Be practical. The bride may know someone who wears the same dress size and can lend her wedding dress to her. It could be altered for the occasion with different ribbons or buttons, a lace or net overskirt, or a different bustle. Also, it's easy to rent wedding dresses at substantial savings.

Sam, the pragmatist, recommends that brides spend less on their wedding gown and more on the down payment of their new home. Heidi, the romantic, suggests a longer honeymoon!

It's not what you wear;
it's what you pay for what you wear.

Chapter 20

PROTECT YOURSELF FROM SCAMS AND FRAUD

"The best way to save money is to not lose it."
—Les Williams

Scams and frauds are everywhere these days. They will increase as the economy struggles to stabilize. Some of the saddest stories we've ever heard are of people who lost all of their savings in a scam or fraud. Many scams and frauds target the elderly, but all age groups are vulnerable. The recent Bernard Madoff scandal reminded us that smart, educated, and wealthy people also can fall victim to scams and frauds. Everyone needs to learn to be very cautious.

Ponzi schemes

The financial terrorist Madoff ran what is called a Ponzi scheme. It is an old-time scheme in which the originator pays out large returns to the first few people who participate. As word spreads of the alleged success of the "investment," more people join and more money flows in. This new money is used to pay the earlier investors. The scheme finally collapses when there is not enough money to pay off the later investors. The unlucky investors who come in at the end lose their entire investment.

A chain letter often works in the same way. Those who start the chain might do well, but others lose because the scheme has worn itself out.

You have "won the chance"—to lose

A common scam is someone emailing you or phoning you to say you have won a lottery or a major prize. All is required of you is a small sum for "processing," paying "local taxes," or some other modest expense. Eventually, there are continuous requests for more money. But each time the victim thinks, "I'll just be patient. I have already put in some money, so a little more won't hurt."

Unfortunately, sometimes "a little more" finally adds up to a lot.

In one case Sam knows of, a retired couple participated in such a scam by initially investing only $13. Slowly, they were conned into sinking their entire life savings of $360,000 into the scam. In the end, all they received was a worthless piece of paper.

It's human nature and pride that motivates us to stick with something, even when we are unsure about it. Everyone hates to admit that they made a mistake. You may be tempted to stay in an investment even if you become suspicious that it may be a scam. It's easy to start thinking, "I'll pull out soon. But I'll stay in until I at least get my money back." This weakness in human nature traps gamblers, too.

Be alert to how you may be manipulated by anything that might be a scam.

"Help us rob your bank account" scam

Another scam is the "Nigerian Oil Minister Scam." In this scam, you are contacted by someone who claims to be a relative of someone who has hidden millions of dollars. They offer to share their wealth with you in return for your assistance in retrieving the funds. They may ask for access to your bank account or credit cards. This is how they steal your money.

Almost everyone has received email letters with this kind of scam. Delete them.

"Fake check" scam

Another scam that also may have originated in Nigeria is called, according to the U.S. Postal Inspection Service, "the fake check" scam. In 2007 alone, the federal government seized more than $2 billion worth of fake checks. The authentic-appearing checks are mailed randomly with a letter asking the receivers to deposit the checks into their accounts and wire a lesser amount to the sender. When they do as directed, the checks bounce. Then the bank demands all of the money back from the victims—including the money that was sent to the scammer!

Part two of the scam is to send you an email explaining that you have been victim of a fraud, but they will help recover your lost money. Then they try to convince you to give them your bank account or credit card numbers. Don't fall for this, either.

Learn more at **www.fakechecks.com**, the Postal Inspection Service's website to educate the public about check scams.

"You have an IRS refund" scam

The Internal Revenue Service is warning taxpayers about fake emails claiming that you will receive a refund if you respond with your personal information. Don't ever give your personal information to any unsolicited email request or phone call.

"Start a home-based business" schemes

Unfortunately, the Internet is filled with work-from-home schemes. Many of these offers require a small "deposit" before you can get started in the "business." Often after the deposit is paid, the buyer is given nothing of value but can do nothing about it.

Recognize scams and schemes

Be wary of offers that:

- originate from someone you do not know.
- sound too good to be true.
- come to your attention via email, phone, or classified advertisements.
- are taped onto telephone poles.
- require a deposit or payment from you to get started.
- use words like, "This is not a chain letter/scam/ scheme..."

You must constantly be alert so that you don't become a victim. Sam has been consulted in cases where the victim was introduced to the scam by a relative, friend, or neighbor who were themselves taken in. He has known close associates and friends who vow that the proposition they are presenting to him is totally legitimate. How did they know? One of their friends reportedly had successfully participated.

Each case Sam investigated, however, without exception, was a scam. He also was never able to track down any person who actually had success in any scam, other than those who participated early in a Ponzi scheme. Note that participation in such a scheme is a crime in many jurisdictions and could subject you to prosecution.

Don't be a potential victim

Recently, Heidi almost fell for a scam. She received a phone call offering to reduce her long-distance charges. The cordial caller explained that a rebate was due on her monthly phone bill. They only needed to confirm her name and address in order to process the rebate.

She was transferred to a "supervisor" for verification of approval. Then the supervisor asked her for her date of birth. When Heidi hesitated, she was told "or you can give us your mother's maiden name or the last four digits of your Social Security number." This was the clue she needed and she said, "No way! Don't ever call me again!" and hung up.

Don't toss it all away with "the roll of the dice"

Avoid all scams, including gambling—the biggest scam of all. "Playing the odds," whether gambling or the lottery, is not the way to create financial stability. The best way to win with money is to invest it wisely. Playing games with your money is not investing it wisely.

You may believe in your heart that you can win your fortune through gambling or playing the lottery. But these "games of chance" are guaranteed to be weighed against you. Have you ever wondered why casinos are so large and lavish? It's because gamblers give them so much money!

Don't throw away everything for which you've worked so hard. Statistically, you are more likely to be struck by lightning than to win the lottery. To make it worse, a large percentage of lottery winners go bankrupt. This is because they are inexperienced in handling large amounts of money, and they are vulnerable to scams.

Don't get tricked by "free" stuff

Sometimes scammers just want one thing, your email address or your credit card number. They have creative ways to get them. One way is to offer you "free" merchandise.

Think twice before you accept "free" merchandise offered on television, radio, or the Internet. The item may be "free," but you usually have to pay a shipping and handling fee. How do you pay for it? You guessed it—with your credit card.

You will often be asked to give your email address so you can receive coupons and "valuable updates" (that means, advertisements). If you give your email address to the world, the world will be sitting there, waiting for you every time you check your email.

Also, when you order a product that offers you the first installment or shipment "free," don't forget to call and refuse additional, periodic shipments. They have your credit card number now, so they can continue to ship you and bill you for monthly supplies or installments you don't want and never agreed to pay for. It's a hassle to convince them to stop the periodic shipments and refund your credit card charges.

Protect yourself from identity theft

Ten million people are victims of identity theft every year. You could spend hundreds of hours and thousands of dollars to recover your financial identity. Criminals can run up your credit card balances, empty your bank accounts, and take out loans in your good name. They also can acquire utility services, medical services, and driver's licenses. Losses from identity theft total between $10 and $20 billion annually.

Keep your contact information "under the radar" as much as possible. When a sales associate asks for your email address so they can email discount coupons to you, refuse the offer. Don't sign up for raffles to win cars, timeshares, or other prizes at shopping malls. Your contact information could be sold to spammers and telemarketers.

Your contact and credit card information may possibly be downloaded off of hotel digital "swipe" keycards, so destroy those, too.

Don't release information

Be very protective of your personal information:

- Don't give your debit card number, credit card number, bank account number, Social Security number, or ATM pass code to anyone who requests it via an email.
- Don't post your private information on online forums.
- Don't use your Social Security number, address, birth date, or ZIP code as a username or password for any pass codes.

- Don't download Internet programs or online links from unknown sources. They may contain hidden fraud programs or viruses embedded in the program.

Also be wary of phone calls from a person or a business you don't know. Be suspicious of anyone who asks you to make a purchase over the phone or requests your personal information. If they claim to be calling from the security and fraud department of a credit card company, hang up and call the number on the back of your credit card to verify.

Protect yourself on the Internet

Fraud via the Internet includes "phishing." This is when fake emails pose as a company you have an account with—for example eBay, PayPal, or your bank—and threaten to close your account unless you immediately email them your user name and password on your account. The website or email may appear to be legitimate and secure. They may claim that they want to "verify" your bank statement," give you a prize, or send you a gift certificate.

Legitimate institutions will never ask for your private information, so don't supply it to anyone. Do not click on any links, open any attachments, or even reply to the email. Delete it immediately.

When purchasing online, always log on directly to the website. Shop only on secure websites. Use website addresses that begin with "https." This indicates that your credit card information will be encrypted when it's transmitted over the Internet. Look for the little padlock security icon in the lower right corner. This may indicate that the website is possibly more secure. When you finish making an online purchase, log off that website immediately. If you assign only one credit card for your online shopping, it will be easier to detect if someone else is making charges on that account.

Avoid making online purchases or revealing personal information on your desktop computer or laptop when it is on a wireless connection. This is because nearby computer hackers can tap into your wireless Internet service and steal your information.

Keep all of your passwords top-secret and change them regularly. Use a combination of letters, characters and numbers in the format required by the website. Install anti-virus software and keep it updated daily.

Watch your credit cards

Thieves need the personal information in your wallet. Always know where your wallet and handbag are and exactly what's in your wallet. Make photocopies of the credit cards and identification that you carry with you. That way, if your wallet or handbag is lost or stolen, you can easily cancel your credit cards. Carry only a couple of credit cards and one blank check with you. Leave the rest of your credit cards and your checkbook locked up at home. Carry only necessary personal information with you, such as your driver's license. Never carry your Social Security card or passport.

When you make a purchase with your credit card, make sure your own card is returned to you. Sometimes the wrong credit card may be returned to you mistakenly. Sometimes it is an intentional scam. Also, make sure that you are signing for the correct amount.

When you acquire a new credit card, do not sign the back. Simply write in the signature space on the back of the card: "check ID." This will require the checkout clerk to ask for your photo ID to match the names on both cards. If someone has stolen your card and their photo identification doesn't match your appearance, they might get caught.

Know that "Big Brother" is watching

Banks and credit unions have paid large sums for sophisticated systems that protect customers from fraud and theft by monitoring each transaction closely. If any transaction seems "not right," the transaction can be filed, without notice to the consumer, as a Suspicious Activity Report with the Treasury Department's Financial Crimes Enforcement Network.

Citizens are under very close scrutiny, which is designed to protect them and catch wrong-doers. Unfortunately, this scrutiny also infringes on their privacy.

Guard your mail

Place your outgoing mail in a locked post office box or take it directly to the post office. Make sure that it is not obvious that a check is enclosed. Retrieve your incoming mail as soon as possible. When you change residences, notify your credit card issuers in advance of your new address. Know when your billing statements are due. Thieves can request a change of address for your card and run up charges before you realize it.

Remove your name from marketing lists

Remove your name from marketing lists. The Direct Marketing Association (DMA) notifies its members that they must remove your name from the lists they sell for five years. Go to **www.dmaconsumers.org**. To reduce the amount of unsolicited mail, catalogs, and phone calls from marketers, you can "opt out" by accessing **www.worldprivacyforum.org/toptenoptout.html**.

Use tamper-resistant checks

Purchase tamper-resistant checks from a reputable printer. Don't put your driver's license number or Social Security number on your checks or allow a retailer to write them on the check. Carry checks only when you need them. Store new and cancelled checks safely. When writing checks, use a permanent gel ink that cannot be washed off. One such pen is Uniball Vision Elite. Make sure all gaps are filled in so the amount cannot be altered. Never sign a blank check or credit card receipt.

Use caution at ATMs

Avoid unnecessary trips to the bank, ATM's, and extra ATM charges.

If you must use an ATM, have your card handy before you reach the ATM. Make sure that no one is watching you, or photographing you, as you enter your ID number. Put the money away as soon as you get it. Don't count it until you are in a safe place. If you feel uncomfortable about the people near the ATM, come back later with a friend. Don't use ATMs after dark. If you use a drive-up window ATM, keep your car doors locked and the engine running. Always take your receipts with you. Never talk to anyone, help them, or let them help you while at an ATM.

Here's an alternative to ATMs, if you need cash frequently: Ask your local grocery store to give you extra cash back from your credit card or debit card purchases.

Use a shredder

Don't be an "easy target" for identity thieves who search through trash and garbage dumps.

Shred, don't toss, every document that contains your name, address, and any of your personal information on it. This includes credit card applications, charge slips, deposit slips, billing statements, financial statements, old credit cards, checks, and receipts.

Many sizes and types of shredders are available at office supply stores. They are not very expensive and are worth the peace of mind. The best shredders cut paper in a cross pattern, rather than in narrow strips. They are called "cross shredders."

File complaint reports

If you think that you've found a scam, first check it out on **www.snopes.com.** The website reports on the latest scams that are being circulated.

Report suspicious activity to the Federal Trade Commission (FTC). Forward the original scam mail or email to **www.ftc.gov/spam**. If you believe that you have been the victim of a scam, file your complaint at **www.ftc.gov**.

Check your credit report

You are entitled to a free copy of your credit reports every six months from each of the three major credit bureaus. Contact **www.annualcreditreport.com**. If you use other websites, you may be charged. When you get your report, check it carefully. A recent study found 25% of reports contained serious errors. Contact the credit bureau and clear up the error. Consider signing up at **www.lifelock.com**.

If you are concerned that your identity may have been stolen, you can put a security freeze on your credit reports. This prevents anyone from viewing your credit report. For the latest rules see **www.financialprivacynow.org**.

Get more information

An informed consumer is a protected consumer. Learn more about scams and Identity theft on websites such as:

- **www.ftc.gov/consumers/consumer/alerts/ phishing.html** for more information on phishing scams
- **www.ftc.gov/bcp/conline/pubs/credit/idtheft. htm** for more information on identity theft
- **www.usps.com/postalinspectors** for the U.S. Postal Inspections Service
- **www.usdoj.gov/criminal/fraud/idtheft.html** for the U.S. Justice Fraud Department.

It's not what you know;
it's what you don't know.

Chapter 21

WHERE DOES IT ALL GO?
INFLATION AND TAXES

"There was a time when a fool and his money were soon parted.
But now it happens to everybody."
—Adlai Stevenson

It has been said, "To acquire wealth is not easy, but to keep it is even more difficult." You need to know how to defend your hard-earned funds from factors that erode your wealth. Two of the most powerful factors that erode wealth are inflation and taxes.

Inflation

Understand inflation and plan for it

Inflation is the creeping higher cost of living. It is the increase in the costs of goods and services over time. Quietly, stealthily, inflation takes your money by reducing your purchasing power, so that your dollars don't stretch as far as they used to. If your income remains the same, eventually it won't buy as much as it used to, partly because of inflation. Similar to taxes, inflation is caused by factors beyond your control. These factors include fluctuations in consumer spending, government deficits, energy demands, worker productivity, and wage levels.

Here's an example of how inflation erodes your wealth. Say the inflation rate isn't too high, just 3%. If you had $10,000 this year, next year, it would be worth $300 less, or only $9,700. In thirty years, the 3% inflation would have eaten 59% of your $10,000, or $4,100.

Look at inflation another way: if the inflation rate was 3% every year, what costs $100 today will cost $103 next year and 3% more each year thereafter.

Remember inflation erodes your savings plan. If you save only at the rate of inflation—say 3% per year—you still are just "standing still." You are not really moving ahead or saving.

Taxes

The government taxes the nation's income earners to provide security and social services to its citizens. Frequent changes to the tax laws alter our ability to control our wealth. This variable must always be considered in your savings and investing plan.

Taxes can sneak up on you

Face the sad reality of how taxes affect your money. You may think only of federal income taxes when you think of taxes. Don't forget that we all pay many more taxes than federal income taxes. The additional taxes include state income taxes, sales taxes, excise taxes, Social Security taxes (deducted from your paycheck), and real estate taxes (on property you own). When you add all these taxes together, you may be paying about 50% of your earnings to taxes. That's a huge bite out of your spending capacity!

Don't overlook the fact that you are required to pay taxes on bonuses as if they were income. Immediately set aside the taxes you will have to pay—before you spend what's left.

Also do this for commissions, investment and dividend earnings, and windfalls such as gambling and lottery winnings, prizes, inheritances, and financial gifts.

Taxes drain your income

Someone once asked, only half joking, "Why does a slight tax increase cost you two hundred dollars, but a substantial tax cut only saves you thirty cents?" Taxes are a difficult situation that every citizen has to cope with, like it or not.

We want to explain why taxes take so much of your income. Ready? Here it is: When you buy something for $1.00, it really costs you $1.60. Or you could say that you have to earn $1.60 in order to be able to afford to spend $1.00.

Why is that? It's because of taxes. The $1.00 price you pay when you buy a cheap cup of coffee doesn't take into account the 60 cents in tax that you will eventually have to pay on that $1.00 of your income.

Don't say, "Sixty cents is no big problem." Add a few zeros and it starts to drain your wallet. Sixty cents of a dollar is 60%— more than half. In other words, if you earn $100 you have to pay $60 in taxes, if you earn $10,000 you have to pay $6,000 in taxes, and if you earn $100,000, you have to pay $60,000 in taxes. Now do we have your attention?

Note that this calculation applies to taxpayers (that's all of us) who are in the 38% state and federal income "tax bracket" (that's many of us). Taxes could go even higher in the future. Check with your tax preparer or accountant to find out which combined state and federal tax bracket applies to you. Considering our nation's complex tax laws, the answer may not be simple.

Numbers count, so remember the math

Most people think that if they are in the 38% bracket, they have to earn $1.38 to keep $1.00. We wish that was true, but it's not.

Their math is wrong because it doesn't take into account the tax you have to pay on the extra 38¢. You need to earn 22¢ more to pay for the tax you will have to pay on the extra 38¢ you earn.

Illustration of after-tax income

Let's assume that you are in a combined state and federal tax bracket of 38%.

If you earn $1.60, you will have only $1.00 left:

$ 1.60	(Income before taxes)
x .38	(Tax bracket rate)
$ .608	(Tax paid)

That means, on every $1.60 you earn, you have to pay a little more than $.60 in taxes, leaving you with only $1.00.

$1.60	(Taxable income)
- .60	(Minus the tax, rounded to 60¢)
$1.00	(After-tax income)

You can calculate it from the other direction:

If you earn $1.00, you will get to keep only 62¢ when the combined federal and state income tax rate is 38%.

38% of the total is tax
100 − 38% = 62% (what is left after taxes)

The above figures are rounded to the nearest cent.

Remember: saving is easier than earning

The good news is that every dollar that you save is equivalent to earning $1.60. Decide for yourself. Is it easier for you to go out and earn $160 so you can spend $100? Or is it easier to simply save the $100 (which is equivalent to earning $160)? Obviously, it's easier to save the $100.

Tax avoidance vs. tax evasion

Everyone who wants to truly become wealthy needs to understand the difference between tax avoidance and tax evasion. Tax avoidance is taking advantage of all legal planning methods to reduce your taxes. It is legal to eliminate paying taxes that you are not obligated to pay. A qualified tax preparer or accountant can assist you in reducing your taxes to the legal minimum.

On the other hand, tax evasion is illegal. Examples include not reporting all of your income, misrepresenting your income, or deliberately putting income into the wrong category. Tax evasion is punishable by fines, penalties, and possible imprisonment. None of these would good on your record. In short: don't even think about evading any of the taxes you are legally required to pay.

Most gains are taxed on a federal and state level and sometimes on a more local basis (some cities have income tax). Find out what your income tax bracket is and the effect these taxes will have on you.

Constitutional arguments against paying income tax are scams. Always file your income tax returns.

Tax credits vs. tax deductions

A tax credit is worth $1.00 for every dollar of credit. That means that you are entitled to the full amount of the credit against the tax to be paid. You gain a 100% savings from a tax credit.

A tax deduction merely reduces the amount of income on which you have to pay taxes. The worth of a tax deduction varies, depending on your tax bracket. Consult with a qualified financial consultant or accountant about the difference between tax credits and tax deductions.

Use your deductions

There are many ways to reduce you taxes, including charitable deductions. The tax laws change yearly, so ask a qualified financial consultant or accountant before you plan a charitable deduction.

Make sure you are being tax-wise with your spending, investing, giving, and savings.

In order to receive all the deductions to which you are entitled, keep all receipts for items that result in tax deductions or tax credits. You need to have the appropriate information for the preparation of your tax return. Also, you would be asked to have documentation of the expenses in case of an audit.

Get professional help

Have a tax professional prepare or review your tax return. If you file a simple tax return, tax advice is readily available. Veterans have access to tax services through the Veteran's Administration. Many community-based organizations have tax preparation volunteers or know where to get tax advice for you.

Complicated returns may require review by a qualified accountant experienced in preparing returns. An accountant could save you money by finding deductions and preventing penalties. Be sure to inquire about the accountant's qualifications.

To research qualified accountants in your area, ask respected friends for a referral, look in the yellow pages phone directory, or search online at sites such as **www.searchforaccountants. com**, **www.accountants.com**, and **www.cpadirectory. com**.

It's not if you owe;
it's how much you owe.

Chapter 22

INVESTING WISELY

"Money is like manure; it's not worth a thing
unless it's spread around encouraging young things to grow."
—Thornton Wilder

When you establish the habit of saving, you will be able to start investing what you have saved. Dreams that were out of reach can be attained with a good investment plan. What do you need to do to improve your career and your earning capacity? Plan ahead to create a legacy for your loved ones that lasts for future generations. You can do that by wisely putting your money into real estate, investments, and establishing businesses. You must also protect your investments, your assets, and the value of your income through proper insurance.

Use your money wisely

Use your money wisely and respect it.

Money deserves your respect because it has "magical" powers to multiply and magnetize. Think about it. Money multiplies and magnetizes the good in your life, if good is already happening. The opposite also is true: Money multiplies and magnetizes the bad in your life, if bad is already happening.

Look at an example in which someone receives a large inheritance. If he is already gives to charities, he will increase his giving. The money increases the good. If, on the other hand, he is addicted to drugs or gambling, that's where the money will go. The money increases the bad.

Money is not only magical; it also has wings. Money can fly away in an instant. It can appear and disappear right before your eyes. Money is a form of energy that we give power to and then exchange that power and make its power flow from one person to another, from one entity to another, either for good or for bad. Use that power with care and respect.

Make interest your friend

Interest also is pretty amazing. It works 24/7/365. Is the power of interest working for you? Or is it working for the other guy instead?

The answer is easy if you think about it this way: Interest is working for you if you have investments. It is working against you if have debt. That's because debt takes your money and gives it to others. Earning interest helps you the same way that owing interest hurts you.

Compounded interest takes small amounts of money and makes them grow into large amounts over time. How? By paying interest on the interest. If you save even modest amounts over as little as fifteen to twenty years, that savings can create financial independence for the rest of your life.

Here's the winning strategy: Make interest your friend. Make it work for you, not against you!

Spend on items that increase your wealth

Buy things that will appreciate in value and pay you back. Don't spend all your money on things that decrease in value and require maintenance costs, such as cars and clothes. The two things everyone loves to buy, cars and clothes, start decreasing in value the moment they are purchased. Then they also need to be maintained.

On the other hand, investments such as real estate eventually increase in value over time. Also, real estate can offer significant tax advantages, another way it pays you back.

Another investment that pays you back is your earning potential. You can invest in your career by purchasing advanced training, tools, software, or a wardrobe that increase the possibilities for advancement.

Before you spend, ask yourself if you're buying something that will appreciate in value and pay you back.

Cautiously keep your funds invested

Financial independence can be attained by successful investments. Investing is how you make compound interest work for you, not against you. To invest, you first need to have a small amount of capital. Other books will explain how to expand and leverage your capital. This book explains only how to acquire the funds you need to invest.

Money that is not earning money is losing its value every day because of inflation. When it comes to inflation, it is true that "time is money." Money has to keep working to maintain its purchasing power. Money grows over time if properly invested, even if invested conservatively, because of the power of compound interest.

Let's say you saved $1,000. If you had an opportunity to put it into an investment that produces 6% a year in cash flow and has 4% appreciation, for a total return of about 10%. Ten percent of $1,000 is $100. What would you rather do with $1,000? Spend it on impulse items that may give you temporary pleasure, such as clothes that eventually will go out of style or vacations that eventually will be forgotten? Or would you rather invest it in something that earns you $100 a year on average or more for the rest of your life and you can pass on to your heirs or enjoy later in life?

You could let the $100 compound over time, that is, reinvest the income. At 10% compounded, an investment doubles about every seven years. For a young person with decades of work years until retirement, that $1,000 doubling every seven years might become an asset worth $32,000 or more.

This assumes that the money is invested in a growth asset in which there is no income tax during the growth of the asset. Distributions, if any, may be covered by depreciation. If you don't know how to do this, talk to a qualified accountant or qualified financial consultant.

Avoid risky investments

When you hear about a so-called "hot" investment, here's an easy test. It's called the "Would you want this to appear on the front page of the local newspaper?" test. Another test is the "Would you be proud to introduce your new business partner to your mother?" test.

Could this risky venture you're considering "blow up" and cause you shame? If you are having concerns, stop and reevaluate. Ask many questions. Investigate. If an offer sounds "too good to be true," it probably isn't true at all—and could lead to heartache, financial hardship, and embarrassment.

Choose "hard now, easy later"

Believe in yourself but recognize your limitations. Listen to people who warn you to be careful. They can help protect you from possible risk. There are always difficulties of some sort with every plan of action, so anticipate them. Know that you will have to make some sacrifices and accept some discomfort and inconvenience along the way in order to make your efforts pay off.

Sometimes a beneficial opportunity is worth a great deal of effort. It may be worth a bit of pain now, for greater gain later. A small amount of "hard" now can result in a lot of "easy" later. The reverse is true, too—a small amount of "easy" now can result in a lot of "hard" later.

Remember: timing is everything

Always be prepared for opportunity. You never know when it might appear.

Several years ago Sam met a young man seated next to him on an airplane. The young man shared with him that he had a great idea for a business, but no capital. Many business owners start out adequately capitalized but waste their funds in the early stages of the enterprise. When they reach their growth period, they have run out of cash and run into trouble. Fortunately for the yound man, Sam offered to fund his enterprise if his business plan proved to be solid.

Sam's new partner started working out of his apartment, with one truck. Now he has more than seventeen trucks. The business has grown from breaking even at $600,000 in sales the first year, to now over $3.5 million, with a profit margin of over 15%.

Both Sam and his new partner were prepared for the opportunity when it came to them. Through good timing, they took a small start and turned it into big gains.

Don't overlook your long-term perspective

Does your budget have an "end-game"? What are you saving for in the long run? You can't reach your goal until you know what the goal is.

One way to get an overall perspective on your finances is to use a process called LEAP. LEAP stands for the Lifetime Economic Acceleration Process. LEAP practitioners in your area can meet with you at no charge to integrate your finances and coordinate your overall strategy. They can help you achieve your full financial potential using a computer simulator that explores all of your options and verifies the outcomes, free of any bias or opinions. We believe that LEAP is an excellent way to strategize your financial future. You can find out more about LEAP at **www. leapsystems.com**.

Understand your home as a debt

The biggest debt that most people have is their home loan. Your home is your castle. Hopefully, you didn't buy more castle than you can afford.

You may have assumed that the value of your house would never decrease. Maybe you were hoping that your income would increase so that you could afford higher payments. Maybe you forgot to add in the cost of maintenance, insurance, taxes, and other expenses on your house. For whatever reason, you may own a home that is stretching your budget beyond what you can affort..

Hang onto your home

If you bought your home with an adjustable-rate mortgage (ARM), the interest rate on your loan may reset to a higher rate. If you have an ARM, make an appointment as soon as possible with your home loan provider. Assure them that you will work with them closely to keep your home. Get a printout of your reset mortgage estimate, including what your new monthly mortgage will be and when it will start. If the reset rate is higher, you will have to pay more each month to keep your home. Start preparing for this new expense immediately.

If you have good credit and want to avoid the uncertainty of adjustable interest rates, you can try to refinance your home with a fixed interest rate. In a time of tight mortgage credit, however, this can be more difficult to do. If you need to refinance and you can't find a new loan, ask your lender for help. Document your efforts.

Avoid foreclosure

Many homes across the country are going into foreclosure. If you are afraid that you can no longer pay your home mortgage, you may be facing foreclosure, too. Whatever you do, try to stay in your home.

Here are some online resources to help you prevent foreclosure:

- **www.hud.gov/foreclosure** (800-569-4287). HUD is the U.S. Department of Housing and Urban Development. This site lists HUD-certified credit and foreclosure prevention counseling agencies.

- **www.housing.org** (888-331-3332). Project Sentinel is a local HUD-certified counseling agency.

- **www.nhssv.org** (408-279-2600). Neighborhood Housing Services Silicon Valley is another local HUD-certified counseling agency.

- **www.homeloanlearningcenter.com**. Mortgage Bankers Associations Home Loan Learning Center has information under Your Finances, then Foreclosure and Delinquency.

- **www.995hope.org** (888-995-HOPE). This is the site for Homeownership Preservation Foundation.

Save on your property insurance

You may be able to save on your property insurance. Property insurance companies often sell their client data to each other. If this happens to you, you could possibly be charged higher rates and offered lower coverage due to a previous claim. An "insurance score," similar to a credit score or rating, is often assigned without the client's knowledge.

Find out what your insurance score report says and if it includes any errors. Request your free copy at **www.choicetrust.com** and **www.iso.com** (under the link "useful features").

Save on your property taxes

You may be able to save on your property taxes. If your home has dropped in value, you may be able to petition your county tax board to reassess your home and tax you at its current, lower value. File the request for reduction in your property tax assessment by contacting your county assessor's office. They will ask you a few simple questions such as your contact information, parcel number of your house, and your estimation of what the current value of your house might be. It's not necessary to hire someone to file the request for you.

Understand assets versus liabilities

To put it simply, some assets are possessions that add to your wealth. (Let's call them "cows," because they give milk.) Other assets can actually take wealth away. (Let's call them "alligators," because they take a big bite out of your income.) Some possessions look like cows, but actually, they are alligators.

An example of an alligator is your car. Yes, a car is considered an asset, because it is something you own. But it is not a real cow because it doesn't increase in value or create money for you. The exception would be if you are in the taxi or limousine business. Your car is like an alligator because it costs you money to maintain it and fill it with gas. Also, the value of the car decreases with every year and every mile.

Your home is probably increasing in value as a long-term investment. In that way, it's an asset, or a cow. But you have locked up a large investment of your funds into your home. There is a "lost opportunity cost" on that money. (Lost opportunity cost is the cost you "paid" because you couldn't invest the money in other ways that might have earned more profit.) Also, your home consumes income for maintenance, improvements, taxes, insurance, etc. In that way, your home is a liability, or an alligator.

The goal is to have cows that give back, not alligators that take away. Another example of an alligator is renting your home, rather than buying it. Renting is seldom good use of your money. You are paying your rent out every month and getting no profit back.

In these changing times, it pays to ask long-term questions about real estate. When it comes to buying a home, be sure to look at all of the options for your funds. What else could you do with the money instead of investing in a home? Are you sure that the home value is going to increase faster than the money you could make if you invested it somewhere else? See the Suggested Reading List at the end of this book and Robert Kiyosaki's book, *Rich Dad, Poor Dad* for more thoughts on this.

To recap, choose cows that beef up your wallet, not alligators that chew it up.

It's not the alligators;
it's the cows that create wealth.

Chapter 23

FOLLOW THE PRINCIPLES OF FINANCIAL INDEPENDENCE

"Life is not about having and getting,
but about being and becoming."
—Matthew Arnold

A Silicon Valley billionaire named David Cheriton made his fortune as a professor when he offered to nurture the concept of a start-up company, even though it had an odd name. The name of the company? Google. Cheriton attributes much of his success to "resourceful use of economic goods and services in order to achieve lasting and more fulfilling goals."

We like his belief that resourcefulness and fulfillment are part of the big picture. Over the past fifty years, Sam has been resourceful in achieving financial independence. This has allowed him to pursue increasingly fulfilling goals. If you learn resourcefulness by following Sam's principles listed below, your life will become richer and more fulfilled, too.

Sam's Principles of Financial Independence

1. **Daily choices add up.** How you spend your money now determines what you will have in the future. It takes many "daily" bricks to build the financial fortress that will protect you for a lifetime.

2. **Small savings over a long time creates more wealth than big risks.** Slow and steady wins the race. The turtle will outrun the hare. Small savings continuously made over a period of time are more likely to create substantial wealth than taking big risks. Remember the miracle of compound interest.

3. **Pay yourself first**. Your savings should be your primary goal. To make sure that your savings account gets paid, pay it first. Take your savings portion off the top of your income, not the bottom of your income.

4. **Separate wants from needs**. Concentrate on needs. Distinguish between wants and needs. Until you're financially independent, concentrate solely on needs.

5. **Toxic debt is poison**. It constricts your financial wellbeing by burdening you with interest payments and dependence on further debt. Toxic debt also prevents you from investing and achieving your financial goals.

6. **Credit is for emergencies**. Pay cash until you reach your goal. Until you are financially independent, use credit only for emergencies. Only buy that for which you can pay cash.

7. **Windfalls are capital, not income.** Capital is for wealth investment. Surplus cash and windfalls, such as bonuses, commissions, inheritances, winnings,

financial gifts, etc., are capital, not income. Capital is for investments that produce income.

8. **Never take a risk or purchase an item you cannot afford.** Calculate if the risk or the purchase will keep you awake at night. Remember, if you are careful now, you will be able to afford more things you want eventually.

9. **Put your own oxygen mask on first.** When it comes to giving, put your own oxygen mask on first. You can't help others if you're not okay yourself.

10. **Inexpensive gifts can show you care.** Expensive gifts can give a false impression and can be motivated by insecurity. The purpose of a gift is to show thoughtfulness. Don't give expensive gifts for the wrong reasons. What is considered expensive depends on your income.

11. **Enjoyment of luxury is brief.** But the anxiety of debt lasts. The pleasure derived from buying a luxury item is short-lived, usually just a few days or weeks. But the anxiety and insecurity caused by the debt go deeper and last longer.

12. **Get fulfillment from personal relationships, not material things.** Love people and use things; don't love things and use people.

13. **Why are you shopping? Know the reasons.** This will help you make better decisions. Don't shop because you feel bored, lonely, or insecure.

14. **Resist the urge to indulge in instant gratification. Invest instead.** Resist seeking satisfaction from impulse purchases, even if they are small. Whenever the desire strikes, pay down debt or set the amount aside to invest instead.

15. **Ask, ask, ask for what you want—and be clear.** You never know how someone will respond to your requests. A manager may give you a discount. Your spouse/significant other may fulfill your desires. Make your needs known; you may be surprised.

16. **Comparison shop first.** Check out the competition. Make sure you are getting the best value and what you really want for the funds you have available.

17. **Buy wholesale whenever possible.** Make the slightly longer trip to a wholesale district or a discount store. Depending on what the item is, the savings can be significant.

18. **Do not buy labels. Buy value.** What you want to buy is quality and value, not status. Items don't increase in value just because they have a designer label. This holds true for clothes, jewelry, furniture, tableware, linens, and cars.

19. **Buy pre-owned whenever appropriate.** A new car loses thousands of dollars in value the moment it is driven off the dealer's lot. Few people notice whether an item is pre-owned or not. Also, you can often get better quality at a much lower price at garage sales, thrift stores, consignment stores, and auctions.

20. **Keep price tags, receipts, and packaging.** Keep original packaging, receipts, and price tags on each purchase to keep your options open. Perhaps the item is defective, doesn't fit your needs or costs more than you can afford. You may even find the same item or a better item soon at a lower price.

21. **Keep your funds invested and working for you, but cautiously.** Money that is not earning money is losing its value every day because of inflation. Money

has to keep working to maintain its purchasing power. Money properly invested, even conservatively, grows over time because of the power of compound interest.

22. **Income $1.00; Spend 99¢ = happiness; spend $1.01 = Misery**. If you spend less than you earn you will be happier. If you spend more than you earn you will become anxious. Overspending puts you into debt. Before you know it, you're working in the future to pay for things that you enjoyed in the past.

23. **Buy what pays you. Don't buy things that decrease in value or cost to own.** What pays you back are financial investments that increase in value and investments in yourself. This includes education, training, wardrobe, tools, and equipment to advance your career. Don't invest in things that don't increase in value, advance your career, or pay you back.

24. **Immediately set aside for taxes**. Do not forget taxes when you get a windfall or surplus cash such as a bonus, winnings, inheritance, or financial gift. Immediately set aside the amount required for taxes.

25. **Personal purchases cost you 60% more because they are after tax**. This is the 60% rule: you are actually paying 60% more than the stated price because you are buying with your after-tax income.

26. **It's not how much you make—it's how much you keep.** We all have heard of people who make a lot of money but don't have anything. Some people who have modest incomes can become very wealthy by hanging onto their money.

Below is a shorter version of these principles. We urge you to copy this list and post it on your bathroom mirror, your refrigerator, or your car visor. Read the list every morning and evening until they become a permanent part of the way you live.

Sam's Principles of Financial Independence

1. Daily choices add up.
2. Small savings over a long time create more wealth than big risks.
3. Pay yourself first.
4. Separate wants from needs. Concentrate on needs.
5. Toxic debt is poison.
6. Credit is for emergencies. Pay cash until you reach our goal.
7. Windfalls are capital, not income. Capital is for wealth investment.
8. Never take a risk or purchase an item you cannot afford.
9. Put your own oxygen mask on first.
10. Inexpensive gifts can show you care. Expensive gifts give a false impression and are motivated by insecurity.
11. Enjoyment of luxury is brief. But the anxiety of debt lasts.
12. Get fulfillment from personal relationships not material things.
13. Why are you shopping? Know the reasons.
14. Resist the urge to indulge in instant gratification; invest instead.

15. Ask, ask, ask for what you want—and be clear.

16. Comparison shop first.

17. Buy wholesale whenever possible.

18. Do not buy labels. Buy value.

19. Buy pre-owned whenever appropriate.

20. Keep price tags and receipts.

21. Keep your funds invested and working for you, but cautiously.

22. Income $1.00; Spend 99¢ = happiness; spend $1.01 = Misery.

23. Buy what pays you. Don't buy things that decrease in value or cost to own.

24. Immediately set aside for taxes.

25. Personal purchases cost you 60% more because they are after tax.

26. It's not how much you make—IT'S HOW MUCH YOU KEEP.

CONCLUSION

Now it's time to close the circle. We began this book with your personal relationship with money and your money relationships with others in your life. Then we looked at factors in your world that affect your money. In closing, we want to circle back to your own life. We're asking you to take a close look at how your life relates to "the big picture."

This book is designed to help strengthen your determination to reach financial independence. When you become financially independent, you won't be so focused on obtaining and spending money. Instead, you'll be freer to focus on what really matters in your life and where your life fits into the rest of your world.

Plan to use your money to create a truly meaningful life. Who would you like to become? What would you like to do to make a difference, if money was no longer a concern?

When you gain financial independence, you start to realize that the world isn't "all about you." Take a moment to think about those around you who would help if you had a bountiful supply of funds. Visualize what you could do to improve lives and make the world a better place.

As Winston Churchill said, "we make a living by what we get, but we make a life by what we give." Resolve to hang onto your dough--and then make your dough rise to help yourself and others!

Remember to visit our website **www.TheSmartestWay. com** often for tips, encouragement, updates, and a provocative blog. Please email us and tell us how you are living *TheSmartestWay™*!

Remember....

It's not how much you make;
  It's how much you keep.

It's not your income that makes you rich;
  It's your savings habits.

It's not what your money makes of you;
  It's what you make of your money.
It's not how much you own;
  It's how little you owe.

It's not the "have-to"s or "want-to"s;
  It's the "need-to"s.

It's not what you do;
  It's how you do it.

It's not your habits that control you;
  It's you who controls your habits.

It's not the wishing;
  It's the doing.

It's not the credit card that is the master;
  You are the master.

It's not what you start with;
  It's what you end with.

It's not what you spend together;
  It's how you spend together.

It's not how much you spend for your children;
  It's how much you care for your children.

It's not how much you spend on a gift;
  It's what you give and how you give it.

It's not what you own;
  It's who you are.

It's not what you drive;
  It's what you pay for what you drive.

It's not your wealth;
  It's your health.

It's not how much you spend for fun;
  It's how much fun you have.

It's not what you buy;
  It's how you shop.

It's not where you shop;
  It's what you get.
It's not what you wear;
  It's what you pay for what you wear.

It's not what you know;
  It's what you don't know.

It's not if you owe;
  It's how much you owe.

It's not the alligators;
  It's the cows that create wealth.

About The Authors

Sam Freshman has dedicated his fifty-plus-year career to being an attorney, banker, business owner, real estate developer, investor, author, and lecturer. Sam is chairman of Los Angeles-based Standard Management Company, which he formed in 1961. His company manages hundreds of millions of dollars worth of real estate assets and business enterprises.

Sam has offered hundreds of hours of consulting to high-income earners and families on how to save and invest wisely. He also provides a special mentoring/coaching program for MBA students at University of California Los Angeles and University of Southern California, on principles of financial independence and success.

Sam, a graduate of Stanford University and Stanford Law School, wrote *Principles of Real Estate Syndication*, (3rd Edition, 2006, Beverly Hills Publishing Company). It is considered the landmark work on the subject.

He has been Adjunct Professor of Real Estate Law at the Graduate School of Business at University of Southern California. He has lectured extensively on real estate investments at Stanford University, Pepperdine University, University of Southern California, University of California Los Angeles, Bar Associations, and CPA Societies.

Sam has four daughters and seven grandchildren and lives with his wife Ardyth in Beverly Hills, California. You can learn more about Sam at **www.standardmanagement.com** and **www.syndicationideas.com**.

Heidi Clingen has twenty-five-years of experience in helping consumers find value. Her expertise has been honed in public relations, retail, editing, teaching, and coaching her clients. Her journalistic experience includes staff titles and editor positions at fashion trade and consumer publications including *The Apparel News Group* in Los Angeles and *The Wall Street Journal* in New York, where she received a Dow Jones Foundation Fellowship.

Heidi holds a bachelor's degree in journalism, magna cum laude, from San Francisco State University; a certificate in grant writing from The Grantsmanship Center Institute in Los Angeles; and a certificate in screenwriting from University of California, Los Angeles. She has been an adjunct professor at Woodbury University and Loyola Marymount University. Recently, she has devoted her time to researching, writing, and speaking on how to live well on a modest income.

Heidi has two sons and lives with her husband Bill in Valencia, California. You can learn more about Heidi at **www. allwritey.com**.

Our Mission Statement
For TheSmartestWay To Succeed Series™

*To help you find smarter, easier ways
to succeed in all areas of your life.*

A Note To Our Readers

Dear Readers,

Success takes a great amount of time and effort!

That's why we are creating *TheSmartestWay*™ to Succeed Series™. Our easy-to-read books are filled with quick chunks of powerful things to think about and tips you can start using today. There's something for everyone in every book!

We want you to succeed in life *TheSmartestWay*. Has this book been helpful? We want to hear from you. Please email your comments to: **Heidi@TheSmartestWay.com**.

May true success be yours,

Sam Freshman and Heidi Clingen

Be a part of our next book!

We are creating
the second volume of this book!
Please email us your favorite tips
on how you save money!

If we use your suggestions in our next book,
we will send you two free copies!

Want us to speak to your group?

We create customized workshops for groups
to learn how to live *TheSmartestWay*™!

Want to meet us in person?

We offer confidential, private coaching sessions
to help you live *TheSmartestWay*™!

Want to contact us?

We can be reached at:
Heidi@TheSmartestWay.com
(888) 524-8833

Want to invest your savings?–Read this book!

Principles of Real Estate Syndication (3rd Edition)

By Samuel K. Freshman

Known throughout the real estate industry as the definitive how-to guide, *Principles of Real Estate Syndication* is filled with examples and illustrations of all aspects of buying property with others. This reference guide thoroughly explains the theory and practice of this time-honored way to invest in real estate.

Here's a sample of more than twenty "five-star" reviews on **www.amazon.com.**

"...This book could be titled, how to build a real estate empire. The book provides practical information and advice on avoiding common mistakes...."

"...Comprehensive and authoritative, a must-read for anyone who contemplates investing in a syndication or becoming a syndicator ...A treasure trove of information...."

"...A hands-on book, well-written, easy to comprehend, and offers the reader a strategic insight into a complex business form ... Should be a permanent fixture in every office...."

"...This is the instruction manual for this type of venture—a compelling synthesis of practical and technical advice and legal analysis. I recommend the book to anyone involved in real estate or other syndications—attorneys, accountants, bankers, investors, syndicators, students, and more...."

"...If you are serious about making money in real estate, read this book. ... This book explains in simple and easy-to-understand language the preparation, execution, and practices that must be taken to become successful in the field...."

"...I truly believe this book, if properly followed, can make anybody who reads it substantial amounts of money .... There are dozens of real estate investing books out there, but this is clearly the best I've found...."

Sam has a distinguished career in real estate and law, as an advisor, developer, and investment partner. He is past Chairman of the Legal and Accounting Committee of the California Real Estate Association Syndication Division. He assisted in the preparation of the California Corporation and Real Estate Commissioner's syndicate regulations. In 1961 he formed Standard Management Co., which has sponsored hundreds of millions of dollars of investments in real estate projects throughout the country.

You can purchase *Principles Of Real Estate Syndication,* 3rd Edition at your local bookstores, or on **www.amazon.com**, **www.barnesandnoble.com**, **www.borders.com**, or **www. syndicationideas.com**.

SUGGESTED READING

BUDGETING:

1001 Ways to Cut Your Expenses, Jonathan D. Pond, Dell Publishing, a division of Bantam Doubleday Dell Publishing Group, New York, New York, 1992.

365 Ways to Save Money, Lucy H. Hedrick, William Morrow & Co., New York, New York, 1994.

Financial Fitness in 45 Days: The Complete Guide to Shaping Up Your Personal Finances, Lorayne Fiorillo, Entrepreneur Media Inc., Irvine, California, 2000.

Getting the Most for Your Money: How to Beat the High Cost of Living, Anthony Scaduto, Paperback Library, a division of Coronet Communications, Inc. New York, New York, 1977.

Life without Debt: Free Yourself from the Burden of Money Worries Once and for All, Bob Hammond, Career Press, Franklin Lakes, New Jersey, 1995.

Save Your Money, Save Your Face, What Every Cosmetics Buyer Needs to Know, Elaine Brumberg and Julie Coopersmith, Facts on File Publications, New York, New York, 1989.

Secondhand Is Better, Douglas Matthews, Suzanne Wymelenberg and Susan Cheever Cowley, Arbor House Publishing Co., New York, New York, 1975.

Straight Talk on Money: Ken and Daria Dolan's Guide to Family Money Management, Ken and Daria Dolan, Simon & Shuster, New York, New York, 1993.

Take This Book to the Hospital with You: a Consumer Guide to Surviving Your Hospital Stay, Charles B. Inlander and Ed Weiner, People's Medical Society, Allentown, Pennsylvania, 1993.

The Expert Consumer, A Complete Handbook, Kenneth Eisenberger, Prentice Hall, Inglewood Cliffs, New Jersey, 1997.

MONEY AND RELATIONSHIPS:

If I Think About Money So Much, Why Can't I Figure It Out? Understanding and Overcoming Your Money Complex, Arlene Modica Matthews, Summit Books, New York, New York, 1991.

The Advisor's Guide to Money Psychology: Taking the Fear Out of Financial Decision-Making, 2nd Ed., Olivia Mellan with Sherry Christie, Investment Advisor Press, Shrewsbury, New Jersey, 2004.

The Seven Stages of Money Maturity: Understanding the Spirit and Value of Money in Your Life, George Kinder, Delacorte Press, a division of Random House, New York, New York, 1999.

Women, Men & Money: The Four Keys for Using Money to Nourish Your Relationship, Bankbook and Soul, William Francis Devine, Jr., Harmony Books, a division of Crown Publishers, Inc., New York, New York, 1998.

WOMEN AND MONEY:

Power Tools for Women in Business: 10 Ways to Succeed in Life and Work, Aliza Sherman, Entrepreneur Media Inc., Irvine, California, 2001.

What Every Woman Should Know about Her Husband's Money, Shelby White, Turtle Bay Books, a division of Random House, New York, New York, 1992.

INVESTING:

Rich Dad, Poor Dad: What the Rich Teach Their Kids About Money—That the Poor and Middle Class Do Not! Robert T. Kiyosaki with Sharon L. Lechter, C.P.A., Warner Books, New York, New York, 1998.

The Only Investment Guide You'll Ever Need, Andrew Tobias, Harcourt Books, Orlando, Florida, 2005.

MAGAZINES:

Barron's
www.barrons.com
Best Life
www.bestlifeonline.com
Better Homes & Gardens (family money section)
www.bhg.com
Business Week
www.businessweek.com
Consumer Reports
www.consumerreports.com
Forbes
www.forbes.com
Fortune
www.cnnmoney.com
Good Housekeeping
www.goodhousekeeping.com
Kiplinger's personal finance
www.kiplinger.com/magazine
Money
www.cnnmoney.com
Real Simple
www.realsimple.com
Shopping Smart
www.smartshoppingmag.com
Smart Money
www.smartmoney.com
USA Today
www.usatoday.com/money
US News & World Report (money and business section)
www.usnews.com
Worth
www.worth.com
Young Money
www.youngmoney.com

MY PERSONAL ACTION PLAN

I will **START**:

_____
_____
_____
_____
_____
_____
_____
_____

I will **STOP**:

_____
_____
_____
_____
_____
_____
_____
_____

I will **RECOMMEND** to others:

_____
_____
_____
_____
_____
_____
_____
_____

A Special Offer for Our Readers

"Thank You" for reading this book! We'd like to offer you:

Free Weekly eTips!

Every week, you'll receive our motivational blog.
TheSmartestWay™ to Succeed
~your weekly coaching message from Sam and Heidi to help
you stay on track toward your goals!

A Year's Worth of Freebies!

Throughout the year, you'll receive goodies and updates
~helpful materials to encourage you, your friends, and family to
live *TheSmartestWay*™!

Ready to grab your **free** gifts? Get yours today!

Simply click on: **www.TheSmartestWay.com**

or emal: **Tips@TheSmartestWay.com**

or fill out and fax this form to: (661) 255-6451

Name _____

Email Address _____

Where did you find this book? _____

Give the Gift of MORE MONEY

for Your Family, Friends, and Colleagues!

_____✓_____ YES, I want _____ copies of

TheSmartestWay™ to Save

at $16.99 each plus $4.95 shipping per book ($21.94 total per book)

California residents: add $1.57 sales tax per book ($23.5 total)

Please allow 7 days for delivery.

My check or money order for $ _____ is enclosed.

Name: _____

Address: _____

City/State/Zip: _____

Phone: _____

Email: _____

Please make your check payable to:

Straightline Publishers, LLC

25876 The Old Road, #313
Stevenson Ranch, California 91381

For volume discounts, contact us at:

Sales@TheSmartestWay.com

(888) 524-8833

INDEX